TRUE LIFE TESTIMONIES OF
VICTORY OVER
DRUG ADDICTION

THEY OVERCAME...

BY
RICHARD E. OMOHUNDRO, JR.

WITH
DAVID HAZARD

Copies of this book can be obtained through:
Teen Challenge New England Regional Headquarters
1315 Main Street
Brockton, MA 02301
(508) 586-1494

Published by TCNE Publishing, 1315 Main Street, Brockton, Massachusetts 02301

Second edition 2003

Produced by Hazard Communications, Inc., P.O. Box 568, Round Hill, Virginia, 20142
Phone: (540) 338-7032 Email: Exangelos@aol.com

All proceeds from the sale of this book are assigned by the author to further the work of Teen Challenge International New England.

ISBN 0-9710804-0-2

THEY OVERCAME...BY THE BLOOD
OF THE LAMB AND BY
THE WORD OF THEIR TESTIMONY.

(Revelation 12:11)

This book is dedicated to all the Teen Challenge staff and students around the world who overcame by the blood of the Lamb.

Contents

ACKNOWLEDGMENTS

Sincere thanks to:

Teen Challenge New England staff and students. Thank you for sharing your stories. You are living proof that there is hope and deliverance from the bondage of addiction for those who choose to accept it.

Pastor Bob Crosby for his guidance and Mt. Hope Christian Center (Burlington, Massachusetts) for their support. My thanks also to Pastor Lou Zinnanti and Christ the Rock Metro Church (Dorchester, Massachusetts) for their support.

Mary Morley, former Executive Member of the Teen Challenge New England Board of Directors, for her project management and editing assistance from first draft to final manuscript. Thanks also to Kate Glennon for her speedy edits to the revised edition.

David Hazard, for the trust and insight he brought to the sensitive work of conducting the interviews for this book.

Richard E. Omohundro, Jr.

Director

Teen Challenge International (USA)
New England Region

FOREWORD

This book can change lives.

The stories told here are not fictional, but true life accounts of individuals who found lifetime freedom from addiction. I personally know most of the individuals portrayed in this book. I can vouch for the fact that their "cure" has stood the test of time. Teen Challenge, an organization that my brother, David Wilkerson, founded, was instrumental in their recovery.

Teen Challenge does not believe addiction is a disease, but a choice and a challenge to be overcome through a faith-based program of rehabilitation. The "faith" that is the basis of the program is not faith in oneself, or in modern professional therapy, but in a relationship with Jesus Christ.

As the debate goes on as to who is most capable of providing help that leads to recovery from addiction, Teen Challenge has demonstrated that true Christian faith produces results that other programs cannot.

I recommend this book for anyone struggling with a life-controlling problem. If someone you know, especially a loved one, has an addiction problem, place this book in that person's hands. It may motivate him or her toward a journey of faith, freedom, and a new life.

Don Wilkerson

Executive Director
Teen Challenge International
World Headquarters

INTRODUCTION

There certainly is no shortage of information on the topic of drug addiction. Stories about drug use, abuse, and treatment appear regularly in print, on television, and over the Internet. News reporters, treatment programs, support groups, researchers, and politicians all weigh in on the subject. Indeed, drug addiction and its attendant social ills have been part of our national consciousness since the 1960s. And with good reasons:

- **Nearly as many Americans die of drug-related causes each year—50,000 dead—as died in the entire Vietnam War.**
- **Since 1980, it is estimated that the U.S. has spent $500 billion on the war against drugs… and the problem is *still* huge.**
- **The enormous cost of drug abuse in 1995 was estimated to be $77.6 billion in lost earnings, $11.9 billion in health care costs, and $20.4 billion in other associated costs.**
- **Cocaine today sells for less than half of its 1981 price of $275 per gram.**
- **Approximately one in four prison inmates is convicted of a drug-related crime.**

Why compile a book about drug addiction? The subject is not often discussed in my everyday business and social life. I am a businessman who returned from the Vietnam War in 1967. Since then, I attended graduate business school and have been active in the investment and finance industry. Most days, I interact with investors, company executives and a cross-section of people in my affluent suburban neighborhood. On a regular basis, I commute into Boston or travel internationally on business. I do not personally know anyone who is currently hooked on drugs. My professional associates, friends, family, and I generally go about our business without thinking much about the cancer of drugs that continually eats away at our society and enslaves entire nations worldwide. We, the respectable citizens and business people of our day, give ourselves permission to remain uninvolved because we mistakenly believe one or more of the following statements:

"The drug problem does not directly affect me."

"Government, politicians, and special interest groups will fight the problem for me."

"Drug abuse is an overwhelming, intractable problem. My involvement cannot possibly make a difference."

While each of these statements sounds reasonable, I submit to you that the problem is too large, too intractable, and too global *to ignore*. My own understanding of this was born almost unintentionally, when in the course of my financial career, I accepted a volunteer position as a treasurer with Teen Challenge. As I became more deeply involved with the ministry, I came to realize the full extent of the addiction crisis, and the full extent of the healing power that individual involvement can bring. Over the past fifteen years of studying drug abuse and addiction, and through my association with some of those whose lives have nearly been destroyed by drugs, I have seen how inaccurate these statements are:

"The problem does not directly affect me."

The sheer size of the problem and its enormous cost to our economy, estimated at **$120 billion per year, affects each one of us**. Imagine what better ways we could spend $120 billion if we already had a successful, cost-efficient way of dealing with the problem of drug addiction. What if we could have back the **$500 billion spent since 1980** addressing the drug problem and instead buy food for the poor, provide health care for the elderly, increase teachers' salaries, and purchase technological tools for our students?

Make no mistake about it, even if you have never been mugged or had your house burglarized by an addict desperate for cash to score his next fix, **this problem affects you directly!**

"Government will fight the problem for me."

I appreciate the efforts of countless treatment and prevention programs. I respect the small cadre of politicians who work diligently and sincerely to establish policies and laws aimed at the elimination of drug abuse in our country. I applaud the heroic activity of law enforcement officers and agencies that daily confront the drug beast. However, the truth is that **government has not, will not, and cannot fix this problem.** Haven't forty years and over half a trillion dollars spent proved that?

"The problem is too overwhelming and intractable for me to make a difference."

Overwhelming and seemingly intractable, yes. Hopeless—never. The truth is, **there is an answer to the problem of drug addiction in America**—a revolutionary answer that stands conventional wisdom on its head. Compared to other methods of combating the problem, it is the most cost-effective and successful answer available, with documented, proven results.

To claim there is proven cure for the drug epidemic may seem preposterous. But if you knew the answer to the problem of drug addiction in America… what would you do with your knowledge? Wouldn't you be eager to share it? Wouldn't you want to help mobilize the resources needed to solve the problem? And I guarantee that your involvement will contribute in a positive, lasting way toward loosening drug addiction's death grip on our nation.

This book will introduce you to some modern miracles: men and women who have overcome hopeless drug addiction. In many cases these people are actively working to rescue others from the walking death of drug addiction. Their success stories uncover a powerful alternative to conventional drug addiction treatment—one that is unmatched by *any* other drug treatment regimen in the world.

WHAT IS THE "WAR ON DRUGS" REALLY ABOUT?

We in the United States like to define a problem in a "sound bite," a clever comment or phrase that reduces a complex concept into a small palatable package just right for media consumption. America's "War on

Drugs" is a great example. It is the moniker ascribed to our government's anti-drug policies and activities. It is a clarion call for activists of all types. And it is the desperate hope of decent citizens who see the spiraling economic, societal, and spiritual toll exacted on us all by the drug problem.

But it is not the answer.

Years ago, I experienced a minor infection. To help cure me, a doctor prescribed a topical medicine. I applied the ointment and nevertheless the condition got worse. The next day I applied it again, with the same results. On the third day, I doubled the dose of ointment and the affected area became very badly irritated. My wife wisely observed, "The medicine is making the problem worse!" When I returned to the doctor he concurred with my wife—I'd had an extremely rare allergic reaction to the iodine in the ointment. When he prescribed another medicine, the original infection was cured quickly.

Sometimes we find answers by looking at problems in a different way.

The Wrong Question

It's my belief that in seeking answers to the drug addiction problem, we are asking many of the wrong questions. One of my graduate business school professors gave us a case-study exam. The assignment was to write all the questions that should be asked about the case. When asked if we should also write the answers to our questions, he said, "No, just write the questions. I will know by your questions if you will be able to reach the right answers."

"Are we winning the war against drugs?" is not the right question. Why? Because drugs themselves are not the core problem. Drugs and drug addiction are symptoms. What is the real problem?

The real problem is the gnawing hunger in the soul of drug users… the deep void they attempt to fill with the numbing high of drugs, instead of learning how to be filled with love for the Creator, love for family and friends, and love for themselves.

Consider the self-destructive life of addicts. They lie, cheat, and steal to feed their inner need. They betray the trust of parents, spouses, children, and employers. They are incapable of loving themselves, and thus incapable of loving others. Most know that a life of addiction will most likely lead to death. Can you imagine any lifestyle that fosters lower self-esteem than drug addiction?

So the real "war" to be fought, the real questions to be asked, are not about drugs, but about the needs of the human soul. Drugs poison the body, while distracting people from their innermost need. Drugs offer only short-term solace, meanwhile provoking an all-consuming appetite for more. Addiction is a dread word, signifying a life out of control, seeking that which does not satisfy, that which only increases bondage to itself.

What Is the Solution to Drug Addiction?

There is no doubt that drugs cause physical and emotional dependency and devastation. However, **chronic substance abuse is primarily a spiritual problem.**

Drug addicts are persons who either cannot find God for themselves, think Him irrelevant to their pursuit of pleasure, or are in open rebellion and defiance of Him. Because this is a problem of the human spirit, it cannot be solved by physical means alone.

A spiritual problem yields only to a spiritual solution.

Therefore, the "War on Drugs" is really a war within each addict. It's a "War on the Spirit." And it can be won only as each individual finds that which is necessary to fill his or her own spirit. That filling is accomplished through a personal encounter with the living God who forgives, heals, and replaces the hunger for drugs with a hunger for Him and His eternal love.

Teen Challenge—It Works

I have found a drug rehabilitation program that gets men, women, and young people off drugs and keeps them off. You won't hear about it in schools or in the media—and certainly not from secular government agencies. And that's really too bad, because it works.

Teen Challenge is the proven cure for the drug epidemic.

Teen Challenge is an international organization that has been working with drug users and addicts since 1958. Its founder, the Reverend David Wilkerson, is well-known and respected around the world, both because of Teen Challenge's irrefutable success and because of his bestselling book, *The Cross and the Switchblade*, which tells the riveting story of how Wilkerson began Teen Challenge in New York City. Today, Teen Challenge has drug rehabilitation centers throughout North America, South America, Europe, Africa, Australia, and the Far East.

More important than the international scope of Teen Challenge is this: While in general, statistics indicate that only two to three addicts out of ten who attend any other drug treatment program get off drugs and stay clean, **Teen Challenge has a greater than 80 percent success rate.**

That's right. For every ten people who complete Teen Challenge's extensive program, which lasts twelve to fifteen months, eight will come off drugs, remain clean, and go on to live new lives. If you compare this with the dismal results of other programs, that's phenomenal success!

What I have learned about Teen Challenge has inspired me to make a major personal commitment of time and energy to this great work. For close to two decades I have been enthusiastically involved with the work of Teen Challenge on behalf of its centers located throughout New England.

In the chapters that follow, seven men and women who have gone through the program tell their own stories. They explain, in the best way possible, how Teen Challenge achieves such amazing success. You'll hear from people who come from very different walks of life. You'll learn how they became trapped by drug use. You'll hear how addiction led some into lives of violence and crime.

These individuals explain in their own words how they were rescued from a dangerous, hopeless way of life. You'll hear how initiating and persevering in a personal relationship with God transformed them, giving them love for God, for others, and at long last, for themselves. Their newfound freedom compels them to tell their stories in the hope of helping others overcome bondage to addiction. These individuals are real. Their testimonies were recorded in interviews with David Hazard. What we present are the transcripts of these interviews, reviewed and approved by the subjects themselves.

You may be a mother or father, businessman or businesswoman, educator or student. Listen to the voices of those who tell their stories in the following pages. Reserve judgment, set aside preconceptions, and reflect thoughtfully on the contents and claims you find inside this book. I want you to know that we do not have to tacitly accept drug abuse, drug addiction, and drug-related crime and death in America. I also want to encourage you. If you know someone who is addicted to drugs, there is hope. There is a way out. There is a proven cure available to those you care about: **a proven cure that works**.

WHAT WILL YOU DO?

After you consider the stories that follow, I believe you will agree that Teen Challenge works. I hope you'll rally with us to remove the scourge of drug addiction from our society. The testimonies of those who overcame—and there are thousands more like them—stand as proof that there is a cure for the drug problem.

The question remains: What will you do to help fight the *real* war on drugs?

CHAPTER ONE

"I NEED A NEW LIFE"

— Jimmy Lilley —

In America's war on drugs, we've seen how our national leaders concentrate a lot of time, money, and energy on fighting the enemy who lies *without.* We're combating drug cartels, importers, regional dealers, and big distributors in our cities. In a way, that's a strategy every one of us tries to use in our personal lives, too. We try to find solutions "out there" to resolve needs and personal conflicts that really lie deep *within* us.

Unless we learn how to win the drug war by discovering how to resolve the longings and conflicts of the individual human heart, I'm afraid all our billions of tax dollars and man-hours of effort will not count for much. Don't mistake me. We should use every means we have to stop the flow of illegal drugs that's destroying our culture. But the right solution is in knowing where the need for drugs begins and how to resolve that need.

What I've learned by observing and working with Teen Challenge is that the drug war—or any other conflict that troubles people's lives—is won or lost in the depths of the human heart. I've seen how inner need, emptiness, unresolved hurt, or conflict hollows out a place inside, and I've seen how good, intelligent people have reached for drugs in an attempt to fill in that hollowness.

That was the case with Jimmy Lilley. Jimmy's moving life story does more than illustrate that an inner need can drive someone to take drugs.

Most of us already know that to be true. The question is, what goes on inside a normal kid like Jimmy Lilley that causes him to cross the line again and again, until he's so deep into drug use that he's a hopeless addict? And what's the first step we need to take when someone is hooked on drugs, even someone who seems beyond hope?

In Jimmy's words, here are the answers.

◆ ◆ ◆

MEET JIMMY LILLEY

Even as a little kid, I knew the world I lived in was a little uncertain. People I loved came and went. Mostly went. By the time I was seven or eight, I already felt these longings for something I could count on.

At night, when I curled up to sleep in the little bedroom in my grandmother's house where I lived, this longing grew pretty strong. My grandma would tell me I was "a good boy." But if I was so good, why had my mom left me and my brother back in North Carolina and gone to live in New York? I knew she was going away to get a better paying job. She'd explained that. But in my heart, I really missed her and needed her. And where was my dad?

I've met a lot of people who feel the same way. Life is uncertain. Who can you rely on? Some of them have followed the same road I was on, using drugs or alcohol to escape a desperate feeling of insecurity that you live with every day. You want life to be good; you want the world to be decent and safe. And it just isn't. You want people to support you and give you what you need. And they don't. Others have tried to escape their insecurity by padding their lives with possessions, career success, and lots of friends. Eventually, most people feel a longing: I need to find a different kind of life. Something secure, dependable, and solid. We all want a way to feel satisfied and at peace on the inside when nothing from the outside can do it.

But where do you find *that* kind of life in an unsettled world like this one? No one could have known by looking at me, "good" little Jimmy Lilley, how many dead ends I'd go down in my search for that kind of life. Or how close I'd come to losing the life I had, before finding the lasting security we all seem to be looking for.

Nothing Settled

It was late May, and in just a couple weeks, grade school would be out for the summer. When I walked in the door with my lunch box, Grandma was at the kitchen counter slicing vegetables for dinner. "There's something for you on the table, Jimmy. And a surprise."

On the kitchen table was a letter addressed to me. I recognized the handwriting on the envelope immediately. It was from my mother, and I eagerly tore it open. Her letters came pretty often, and getting one was the greatest thing. It was kind of like being able to hold her hand or sit on her lap for a while. This one began by telling me about a funny thing that happened to her on the subway and then went on to tell me—for probably the millionth time—to do good in school and obey my grandparents. I skimmed through that and came to the part I was *really* looking for.

At the end of June, when school was out, I'd be going north to stay with her for a few weeks. Me and my older brother, Bobby.

I let out a whoop. I loved going to New York. What a change from quiet North Carolina. Back then, in the mid-1950s, it was *really* quiet. But New York! In my mind's eye, I could picture the skyscrapers and busy sidewalks. The department stores. Maybe we'd go to Central Park, and the zoo. My place was with Mom—it was just that I couldn't be there.

When I put the letter down I must have been beaming. "We're going to New York," I told Grandma. "Is that the surprise?"

Grandma wasn't smiling at all. She wiped her hands on a towel and came to the table. "Sit down, Jimmy."

I pulled out a kitchen chair and sank into it, with my elbows propped on the table. Grandma's normally sweet face was lined with concern. I'd gotten scolded by my teacher for talking in class, but I didn't think the school would call about that...

"Your father is coming to see you."

"When?" My thoughts reeled a little.

Mom and Dad had divorced before I was three. That was when Mom went to New York to work at a job that paid a lot better than anything she could find in North Carolina. Grandma, Grandpa, and my mom's brother were raising Bobby and me. And Dad—well, from things I'd overheard about him, plus the fact that unlike Mom he *never* wrote or called, I wasn't sure I wanted to see him. He was rough, troublesome, barely a step ahead of the law. And he was mean and violent when he drank. I had a pretty good idea that was why my parents were divorced, and had vague images in my head of him threatening and hurting my mother.

"He's coming by tomorrow." Grandma's very southern voice was soft as she studied my face to see how I'd react. It was kind of odd, but I'd already spent enough time away from Carolina, as we called it, that I didn't have the same accent.

"What does he want?" I must have sounded more skeptical or jaded than a grade school kid should sound.

"You don't have to spend but a little while with him," she said to reassure me. "He's your daddy and he just wants to see you and Bobby. He won't stay long."

A whole bunch of feelings were fighting in my chest. I wanted to see my dad—maybe more out of curiosity than anything. I'd only seen him once before, but I was so little I could barely remember it. Why was he coming *now*—when he obviously didn't give enough of a rip about us to be part of our lives? And knowing he had a mean streak, I also felt afraid.

It also stirred a deeper feeling I had—the feeling that I could never count on anything in my life to stay settled. Just when you felt secure, something always happened.

In the end, there was no way around seeing my father.

The next day when my dad showed up at the door, in a work shirt, jeans, and boots, he had the same roughness I remembered. He asked me a few things about school and my friends, but seemed pretty uninterested in the answers. Maybe he felt like he didn't have any business asking too many questions. In some very small way, it felt good to see and hear my real dad. But mostly, I felt cold toward him and uncomfortable. Kind of disconnected.

Truthfully, I can't remember anything of what he said. I was closed to him, and very relieved when he left. He didn't say when we'd see him again, and nobody asked. All in all, the "big surprise" of my father's visit was pretty much a big nothing. Whatever the point of it was, it was lost on me. And yet in another way, it was as if a long fuse had been lit.

For one thing, it only emphasized the tone of my whole life. Inside, I always seemed to carry these huge longings and conflicting feelings. Nothing ever seemed settled. Not that this was a new feeling really, but it was like I was trying to walk through life without solid footing. Trying to figure out what it was that made you important enough for anyone to pay attention to you.

After Dad's visit, my brother and I would go to New York to visit Mom, and then come back to North Carolina. She'd come to see us. I'd keep up this pattern of bouncing back and forth. And on the surface I'd look to my mother and grandparents like the same good kid. But underneath, I was different. Though nobody knew it, not even me.

Something to Count On

Cheap wine is everywhere. It sure was in North Carolina, anyway. Along with corn liquor. I can't remember *not* drinking the two-dollar kind of wine that's sold in smelly little quick-stop grocery stores along the highway. How does a young kid—younger than ten—get hold of alcohol? The answer is friends. Or older kids in the neighborhood. If you were a kid in my neck of the woods, you drank. After dark, and in secluded places. If my mother and grandparents had known, they would have whipped us good. I started well before grade school ended.

Secretly, even as a little kid, I have to say I *loved* the warm glow I got from swigging corn liquor. The burning sensation as it hit the back of the throat was terrible. On my first try, I half-inhaled, and wound up coughing and choking out most of what I took in. But—man, what a sensation! I had no idea that, from my very first experience with "white lightning," I'd taken my first step down a long, dangerous path.

The simple fact was if you *didn't* drink, you didn't really fit in. Not with the cool kids, anyway. Bobby always seemed to fit in.

Instinctively, I knew that fitting in would give me a place to belong. I hated the feeling I got when I felt like I didn't fit in. It added to that deep-down feeling that I was unimportant. When I drank, I fit in and had a place. I could count on drinking as a way to make me feel like somebody. Sad, but drinking cheap wine settled that issue for me. Or so I thought.

Not long after I turned twelve, I rode my bike to one of our usual hangouts. I found my brother with some of the guys. I expected someone to hand me a bottle, but they were too busy passing the stub of a cigarette around. Sometimes we got packs of Marlboros or Salems. Sometimes guys got hold of tobacco and papers from home and rolled them. But usually, everyone smoked their own.

This time, it seemed weird to me that everyone was sharing one cigarette. One guy would take a slow drag, making the tip of the brown rolling paper glow gold-red, then hold his breath for maybe five seconds before exhaling a cloud of blue-gray smoke, and pass the glowing stub along. I'd already been smoking and wanted a drag too. "Hey, gimme a drag," I said, reaching for it.

The guy who'd just taken a puff looked at my brother and held it back. "You want me to give it to him?"

I looked at Bobby, noticing his face for the first time. He had a dreamy smirk and far-off look. "Are you okay, Bob?"

"Sure. Don't worry about it," he shrugged. "I'm just in my own world here, man. It's great."

They tapped him impatiently, pointing to the cigarette—though now I knew it wasn't your ordinary cigarette. "You want him to have a drag?"

"This ain't a regular cigarette, Jimmy," my brother said, his eyes very glassy and his voice a little hoarse. "This'll get you high. It's marijuana. You want to try it?"

I felt a small thrill of daring go through me. This was 1960, and marijuana was around, but not exactly everywhere like it would be in a few years. Probably someone here swiped a couple "reefers" off their older brother. If drinking was edgy, smoking pot was way over the edge. The adults would kill us if they knew. *Of course* I wanted a drag.

I nodded.

But my brother hesitated before giving the other guy the nod. Impatiently, the other guy elbowed him. "Hey—you *in* there?" Still, Bobby hesitated—just long enough that I felt a pang.

What if he said no? It was like the group we hung out with, and my brother, had moved on to a new place and I'd been left behind. I started to feel like a stupid little kid. A nobody. What if they left me out?

"Sure. Go ahead," Bobby said finally.

I was relieved. When the glowing stub of rolled paper was handed to me, it was like I'd been admitted to an exclusive club. I took a drag. I didn't have a clue that a single, simple puff was my gateway into a whole new world.

Not that this was the first time I'd heard about drugs, of course. The so-called "beatniks" were making headlines for turning the world on to pot and other drugs. Our school had also held an assembly featuring a guy named Nicky Cruz, who talked about his former life as a New York City gang member and drug user. Nicky was now part of a program called Teen Challenge, and when he wasn't counseling ex-gang members and drug addicts hot off the New York streets, he went around the country warning kids about the dangers of drug use. He'd mentioned the dangers of pot, of course, and went on to tell us more about the terrible devastation of using harder drugs like heroin and cocaine. There were grotesque pictures of emaciated, greasy-looking bums, lying around filthy tenements, sticking dirty needles into bulging veins. There was talk of disease, insanity, and death. I'd been horrified and decided then and there I'd avoid all drugs like the plague.

But here I was squeezing a joint between my lips, with another guy reaching for it. "Come on, you dope. Pass it on."

I passed it, and felt like a big shot. And if I had any memory of those pictures of burned-out, half-dead junkies, they drifted off with the curls of smoke. My eyes were fixed on the faces of my brother and his cool, older friends. All smiles.

I was in. I was not out. Besides that, a feeling of euphoria was coming over me. I felt light-headed. When the next joint came I took longer drags, and held them in, like the other guys did. Pretty soon I was in my own world, too. All light-headed and good feeling.

My place in this little world was secure.

My Own Little World

The world of drug use wasn't so "little" after all. Every time I turned around I met someone else who was into drugs. Even so, I kept my drug use in check for the next couple of years. All through junior high and high school the drinking got heavier. There was lots of beer and white corn liquor. But my drug use was limited to smoking pot.

The thing is, though, once you've crossed the line into drugs, you always meet other people who can open new doors for you. That's the thing I seemed to be looking for. A way to create a world where I just felt good about myself all the time. My own world.

Frankly, I enjoyed smoking pot. I felt euphoric. There were no frustrations, no pain when I was high. I had the usual anxieties, about girls for instance, or what I'd do with my future. When I smoked pot, my thoughts relaxed. I felt at peace. More often than not, I also tended to feel inferior. Using made me feel like part of a superior group that was cool enough to do risky things. And very simply, it was pleasurable. Not that I spent a lot of time justifying it to myself, but once in a while the thought crossed my mind that pot was helping me get through the nerves and pressures of adolescence.

The downside was that my grades suffered. And something else I didn't see at first. The feeling I got when I was high, of being peacefully afloat in my own euphoric world, eventually carried me into another feeling—of being separated from everyone else.

Increasingly, I experienced moments, then days, then a sense that wouldn't leave that I was separate from everyone. Isolated. That was not what people saw, though. What everyone including my grandparents and teachers could see was a "good kid" who loved football, scientific reading, and research. A kid who also had the eye and talent to become a good artist. They couldn't see, and neither could I, that taking drugs was having the slowly devastating effect of making me feel utterly alone and sad even in a crowd. My desire to find a place in the world that was all my own had led me into a world where I felt all *on* my own.

The drugs were having other effects, too.

From the time I'd puffed that first shared joint, I'd been getting pot from my brother. He'd saved some seeds and cultivated a small garden way out behind my grandparents' house. Grandma, respectful of our adolescent need for privacy, gave us enough space that he could secretly package it in bags for sale and store it in a cardboard box. Great for me, because that made it easy to get—and it was free. So I smoked pretty much whenever I wanted.

One afternoon, when I was fourteen, I slipped into Bobby's room, and fished the box out of its hiding place. Just before I did, I eyed the door. Was that a creak of a floorboard? Was someone sneaking up on me?

I'd been feeling a little anxious all day. Everything made me irritated—Grandma asking if I'd done my homework, Grandpa asking if I'd mowed the lawn. When they looked at me, I felt like they were looking *into* me. Reading my thoughts. I suspected they knew we were doing drugs, and were just waiting to catch us at it. Maybe the cops had caught one of the kids Bobby sold to, and told my grandparents—and for some reason I couldn't imagine, they were all toying with us, wanting to catch us in the act. I really needed a joint to calm me down.

But when I took off the lid, the box was empty. Under my breath, I swore. My mouth was dry and I was sweaty. I *needed* to get high.

A short while later, out in the neighborhood, I found someone who sold me a few joints. It took at least a couple joints now to kick open the door to that drifty, euphoric world where I wanted my head to be. And while I prided myself on holding the line at pot, I was unaware that, like it or not, the line inside me was moving.

Among our small crowd, and in the bigger crowd of drug users my brother and I knew, a number of people had moved on to other things. With drugs, there was always a next step. As the mid-1960s came, a whole drug culture was forming. By my junior and senior years in high school, a lot of kids were getting into pills, both uppers and downers. A few older guys I knew had gone hardcore and were shooting the big bad—heroin. By then I'd learned—despite what the school's anti-drug films said—that a few shots of heroin didn't make you an instant addict or kill you. It was one of those so-called "facts" that users snickered at behind the backs of all those dull, goody-goody non-users with their warnings.

One night, not long before high school graduation, I drove around town looking for some good dope. My brother had moved out, and so my free supply was harder to come by. And everywhere I went I seemed to just miss the connection.

Feeling irritated and edgy, I stopped by the apartment of a guy we knew—I wouldn't call him a friend, because I thought of this guy as a dope fiend. A head. He mainlined heroin. Gerald (the name I'll use for him) was a mess. His droopy, runny, red eyes and scarred arms disgusted me. But maybe he knew where to get some good smoke.

As it turned out, he didn't. "But I know exactly what you need," he said, smiling. I noticed his gums, like his face, were swollen and looked very red.

"You need more than those little cigarettes, Jimmy. Aren't you tired of those things by now? You need something that'll keep you up."

"Oh sure," I said, half mocking, "*you* know what I need all right."

He held up a syringe, and in the plastic tube I could see a small amount of liquid. "You'll like this, I promise. Come on, be a big boy. This little needle-stick ain't gonna hurt you. And I promise, after that you'll be feeling no pain."

I can't truthfully say I was in any great pain. The anti-drug stuff tended to paint hardcore users as sad people who couldn't handle their lives. Sure, I'd always lived with that uncomfortable and insecure feeling that I just didn't belong. But I wasn't some sad, wounded guy who'd been beaten up and kicked around by life. I don't know what it was exactly, other than the fact that over the years the "line" I'd held against using hard drugs had just moved.

In the end, it was that fact—plus I really, really wanted to get high that night—that made me give in. But no way was I going to shoot up. Instead, Gerald folded a dollar bill into a triangle and dipped it into a plastic baggie of white powder. I took it from him, held it to one nostril and pinched the other closed and inhaled quickly.

In just seconds, the rush hit my brain—like nothing I'd experienced before. I was flying. Gerald was laughing at me. Even with my head spinning out of control I thought he was stupid and hideous. Just a junkie. But so what if he laughed? I was in a whole new world. I felt like I'd made a step up to a whole new level of being.

In fact, I'd taken a huge step down.

Closing In

The *other* next steps came quickly. For one thing, I got out of high school and immediately moved to New Jersey to live near my mother, who was still in New York, and to find work. Quickly I found a job and a small apartment. Shortly after my first heroin high, I scored another, and another. Then came my first LSD trip. Then speed.

By now, my whole frame of thinking had changed. Even while I was doing pot throughout high school, I looked at hardcore drug users as "those" people—real outsiders. Gradually, using pot had molded my thinking, shifted that inner boundary that had long kept me from crossing over to hard-drug use. Now, every new drug I tried seemed like the next "logical" step to experience different kinds of highs.

My father came to see me at my apartment in New Jersey—the third time in my whole life. He'd just gotten out of prison, and he seemed more like an angry, pathetic alcoholic than before. On and off for the next year or so, he'd move in and out of my apartment, while trying to keep a steady job and get back on his own feet again.

When he was with me, it was crazy. He would drink heavily and slump into a chair, glaring at me with red eyes. Then came the same lecture, delivered in his slurred, loud, and abrasive way.

"If you ever drink I'll *kill* you. If you ever take drugs I'll *kill* you. You got that?"

"Sure, Dad. I got it."

What he didn't know was that I was already in deep. And getting deeper.

Very quickly, I'd discovered that the heroin world was peopled by a whole different breed. These were the people of the night. They were loners. Mysterious. They got their drugs in dark back alleys, or on half-lit side streets where you met guys known only by nicknames. You handed money in through their half-opened car windows and they handed you your "junk."

I am saying "they" here, as if I'm describing other people. But the truth is I was starting to slip into the lifestyle and becoming part of that breed of mysterious and lone junkies.

Somehow, I had the sense to see what was happening to me. I could feel the whole drug thing closing in on me. But then, I was too smart to let that happen to me. I was no drugged-out bum.

Like a fox avoiding a trap, I kept myself out of New York. The New Jersey drug world was one thing. I was meeting more hardcore users all the time. Even some real dope fiends. But I knew that New York would take me over. Once again, I drew a line inside myself and kept myself and my drug habit in New Jersey where I knew I could control it.

At least I hoped I could.

DYNAMITE

In 1968, the war that had been heating up in Vietnam exploded. I was just twenty, and a prime candidate, but the draft missed me. I took a job in a munitions factory—and talk about finding your niche.

I very quickly became an inspector, running tests on 81-millimeter shells destined for Vietnam. I got so good and so fast that I could do the work of three people. Of course, my bosses never knew the little secret of my success: I was high all the time. Speeding. On the weekends, I'd drink or do other drugs, but during the week I was wildfire on the job, thanks to speed.

And so I was, pretty literally, "playing with dynamite." Even though I was making good money, sometimes I'd briefly wonder where I was going in life. My brother came up to New Jersey to live with me. By now, he was into his own things, though. My isolated world was starting to feel very empty.

In fact, I was starting to experience depressions. Not just garden variety "blues." Some pretty dead, empty places. You can believe I fought to distract myself in every way possible from the terrible hopeless nothingness I sometimes felt.

Distractions were not hard to come by. For a little while, while Vietnam reached its height in 1969 and the early 1970s, I found a lot of purpose in protesting the war. The hippie movement was big, and drugs were what was happening. Somehow we managed to legitimize drug use by combining it with the drive to rebel against "the establishment" and with political issues. The rhetoric was that society had made everyone so conformity crazy that you couldn't even think right *unless* you were high. Once again, for a brief moment, I felt part of something big.

During this time, about 1971, I ran into a guy who was just back from Nam. He was doing something I'd never even considered—mixing LSD with heroin. "You gotta try this, Jimmy. It keeps you *up* for twelve hours or more."

So much for my resolve that I was going to "control" my drug use. That thin little line inside me was now like wet tissue paper. I began mixing LSD and heroin—and when I started to come down from that I'd do some speed to get me flying again.

There is not much I can recall about the next three years. I was constantly mixing one combination of powerful drugs after another. It didn't matter that Jimi Hendrix and Janis Joplin died choking on vomit they coughed up during bad heroin highs. To put it mildly, there was no line left in me. I just didn't care.

And yet, even as I say that, speaking about that zone of flat hopelessness drugs creates in you, some small voice inside me was screaming. Screaming for help. *But maybe*, I thought, *I'm too far down.*

Now, thoughts of suicide haunted me every day. In my head, I saw ghostly images of me, lying dead. That little part of me that still wanted to live told me these thoughts were crazy. I'd never wanted to die before. Mostly, I could force these thoughts out of my head. If not, more drugs would drive them out.

But if I could escape the thoughts of suicide, there were other thoughts that caught me by surprise and wiped me out. In my weakness and vulnerability, those old, old feelings came in like a flood. It was the feeling—by now it was a deep-down belief—that there was no security in anything or anyone in this whole world. Sometimes the sadness of this thought overwhelmed me with a flood of incredible sadness.

With the wave of sadness came another thought. Now I thought I knew why I'd felt so insecure all my life: *My life has no value. I'm not worth anything to anyone, and I never have been.*

There it was. A couple of the biggest core issues of my life. I'd always looked for someone, or something, to make me feel like I was worthwhile and that I belonged. Now the voice of utter hopelessness took over. Maybe, it told me, drugs had cleared my mind and revealed the truth—just like the hippies said. Maybe I was seeing at last that I was just a *zero.* And maybe I *shouldn't* go on living.

If I'd been playing with dynamite before, handling these same thoughts in my head every day was absolutely deadly. Drugs had led me into a tiny prison of paranoid, and now self-defeating, thinking. I couldn't see that I was stuck inside my own head. What made me think doing *more* drugs was going to help me out? I had no other answer.

I Was a Dead Man

To suppress the thoughts of suicide, my days spun into an ever-downward cycle of constant drug use. I'd long since quit drinking because alcohol was no longer any escape for me. Instead I'd do heroin, and when I was crashing from that, I'd do speed. On the comedown from speed, I'd do heroin again, and on it went.

The truth is, I'd been wrong to think that inside me there was no line left to move. At first, as I said, I rode the heroin-speed roller coaster to suppress the voice that said: *Just kill yourself and get it over with.* After weeks and months, I realized I was actually overdoing the drugs so that I *would* die.

I haven't mentioned that I had a girlfriend during this time. That's because I was so self-absorbed and drug-focused I might as well not have had one. To her credit, she had the good sense to leave me. But I'd really cared about her. Her leaving was like the death of hope.

At just about the same time, my grandfather suddenly died. Another major blow. Was this what my whole life was about—losing people I loved, and death?

I was rapidly losing it emotionally. Someone I hardly knew called me a junkie. I became enraged and lost control. In a haze, I found myself running up the street, yelling and screaming.

On another day, in the pits of despair, I woke up on my apartment floor. Some guys I knew were banging on the door, trying to find me. I crawled to the toilet, poured all my drugs in the bowl. Inside I was shouting. *I gotta stop,* I thought—not as *just* a thought, but as a desperate prayer to God.

I don't know how long after this I made my way to a local park. Maybe a day, maybe a week. I was utterly lost in every way. In my pocket were hits of heroin and LSD, enough for three heavy trips. Flopping down on the grass beside a tree, I snorted all the heroin and downed all the acid.

The overdoses plunged me into hell. I could hear myself screaming as terrible hallucinations came at me. I could feel myself slowing, like I was a fly getting trapped and exhausted on sticky flypaper, then suddenly I'd be speeding through space. My stomach turned over and over, making me retch until my abdomen cramped violently. The torment went on and on.

Hours into the trip, I felt my whole body cooling. I'd been sweating profusely, and now my fingers and toes, then my arms, then my torso, grew cold. I felt lethargic and weighted down. The growing cold made me shake. Numbness crept up my arms and legs, over my neck and lips. Faintly, I thought, *I'm dying.*

I can't say for sure what happened next—if I actually did die. But I can tell you there came a moment when, as definitely as you feel your hand slip out of a glove, I felt my spirit leave my body. I looked down and saw myself dead. *Too bad,* I thought—but I had no feeling about it one way or another. I seemed to be crossing the last line there is to cross. And my only thought was, *who cares?*

Later I learned I'd laid there in the park for eight hours, while a massive overdose of drugs fought to push me across the line from life to death. By chance, a friend found me and got me to an emergency room. How they saved me, a doctor said, was beyond him.

In my mind, it would have been better if they hadn't bothered. Back out on my own, I knew I was a dead man. I knew I would do it again and the next time it would work. And yet…

Somehow in this pit, a new thought came to me: *I need a new life. But where do I go, and what do I do to get one?* Today, I know that someone heard those thoughts. And not only heard, but answered.

A NEW LIFE

I was back in the park where I'd overdosed. Dismal months of living death had gone by and it was now the summer of 1972. I'd been sitting there under a tree, wrapped in a blanket and strung out for two or three days. Occasionally, people approached me and I'd sell them drugs.

Late one hot August morning, I was nodding off when I had the feeling someone was looking at me. I raised my eyes, and found a nice-looking black lady, probably middle-aged, standing there smiling at me. I smiled back.

"Can I talk to you about Jesus?" she asked. Now I noticed she had a couple of small kids with her. A nice little wholesome troop of "missionaries," out earning a scout badge by talking to a junkie.

Dear God, I thought, *I don't need this.* But I said, "Sure." Maybe I'd mess with her mind a little—then go hardcore on her and get her to leave.

The smile had vanished from her face and she looked me straight in the eye. "Jesus can give you a new life."

Instantly, my own desperate words came back to me. Hers caught me off guard. "*What* did you just say?"

"I said Jesus can give you a new life. He is the Lord of life. He's your maker. And no matter where you are right now, no matter what you've done, He can take your old life away and give you a brand new one."

My mouth must have hung open as she told how I could leave behind the life I was living and receive new life as a free gift from God. I could have this gift if I turned my life over completely to God's Son, Jesus Christ, who had died on the cross in payment for all I'd done wrong.

As she spoke, I couldn't help but think of everything I'd done in my life—every illegal and immoral act, every mean and selfish act. Could God really forgive *all* that, plus the incredible wrong of throwing my life down the toilet?

"When Jesus shed His blood on the cross," she said, as if she knew my thoughts, "His blood covered every sin. All of mine. All of yours." The woman, Dottie, ended by inviting me to come to a meeting at her church that evening. After some half-hearted objections, I agreed.

When I walked in the door of the church that evening, what I walked into wasn't a formal service but a sanctuary packed with people—some praying, some telling what had just happened to them.

The first person I ran into was a guy who had sold me drugs just two weeks before. Something about him was definitely changed, though. I could see it in his eyes. His whole being was changed. As he took my hand, his eyes filled with tears. "I met Jesus here. Man, don't do drugs anymore."

Down at the front of the sanctuary, a woman who'd been kneeling in prayer looked me in the face as she got up. "This is real."

Another guy told me he'd suffered severe hallucinations in which Satan was dragging his soul to hell. Drugs were destroying his mind. "But since I gave my life to Jesus Christ, I got my mind back."

To be honest, it was all too much. God didn't want me. I wasn't worth it. I went home that night and got stoned. In fact, despite the hope-filled words I'd heard, something set me off again. I jumped deeply into chemicals, and the voice of suicide took over again. This time, I was determined to end it by turning on the gas oven in my apartment and lighting a match. Forget life. I wanted death. I'd given up totally.

Right in the middle of my plan, though, a voice—one I'd never heard before—said, *I can help you.* Actually, it occurred to me, I had heard this voice before. I just hadn't recognized it before this moment. *You can have a new life. Don't do drugs anymore. This is real. You can have your mind back.*

It occurred to me that I'd finally come to the end of myself—only to find that when even I had given up on me, God was there waiting with open arms. It felt like He was welcoming me to His side right now, saying, *Come on, let's get your head back together. Let's get your life started all over.*

Shortly, I returned to Dottie's church with her. The minister asked if anyone was lost and my head was nodding. He invited anyone who wanted to walk with God to come to the front of the church for prayer and I just about ran to the wooden rail where people were kneeling.

"Son," he whispered in my ear, "if you want to have a new life in Jesus Christ, pray right now and give Him your old life. Let Him take it away. Let Him fill you with His Holy Spirit—and He'll give you a new kind of life. The kind that's eternal life."

This time, nobody had to ask me twice. I began to pray. And as I prayed, the pastor began to pray for me, and gently laid his hands on my head.

Nothing like this had ever happened to me before. When his hands touched the top of my head, something like electricity went through my scalp and down into the core of my being. I felt new down in my very bones and muscles. At the same moment, it was as if I'd been locked in a dark, dead place, like a coffin—and now the lid blew off and light poured in.

I laughed. I cried.

I knew now it was true. I was wanted by someone. In my lostness, the Shepherd of souls had come to me and reached out a welcoming, healing hand. I knew I had to follow. Unbelievably, I knew I could begin again and experience a new life.

HEALTHY NEW HABITS

For two weeks, I did great. Then I went right back to heroin. I hated it. I also knew the new start I'd been given by God was real. But I needed something to help me stay on the right path.

Dottie knew I needed strong and practical help. She told me about Teen Challenge—that same program I'd heard Nicky Cruz talk about in a school assembly so many years before. Not only would I get good solid teaching from the Bible about the Christian life from them, but they were highly experienced in teaching people how to build the healthy new habits needed to overcome drug addiction.

A contact was made. Yes, I could come. Needing to get away from my home territory, in no time I was on my way to a Teen Challenge center in Philadelphia. For one year, I would work on building a relationship with God and with other people. And I'd work on building healthy new living habits that, for me, would become the pathway to a whole new life.

Teen Challenge worked for me. Why? Probably the first reason was that I was accepted just the way I was when I walked in the door. All my life, I felt like I needed a place to belong. Here, I was another child of God, just like everyone else. The empty longing inside me grew less and less as I knew I had found my place in the world.

There was very practical help, too. As you can imagine, the life of a drug addict isn't very disciplined. We make a lot of promises to ourselves and to other people. We have good intentions, but we easily give in to laziness or the easy way out. We talk big, but feel little and inadequate. We set goals, but never work for them. We say we'll tell the truth, but manipulate facts until we're telling full-blown lies when it would be just as easy to tell the truth. We live in a lot of crooked ways, and don't know how to deal straight.

Teen Challenge gave me the discipline I needed to set me right. They helped me direct my time by scheduling it well. They helped to direct my mind, by giving me good mental work to do, studying and memorizing the Bible. And that, in turn, helped direct my thinking in healthy new ways as the positive words and promises of God sank in.

All in all, Teen Challenge helped me to set high standards for living—God's standards. And in that way, in time, the counselors helped me find the path that kept me, for more than twenty-five years, free from drugs and living the new life I have always longed for. Having God in my life has given me the inner security and solid footing I lacked.

I know now that God has a place in His heart and in His plan for every one of us. He can put you on a sure path if you are lost. And I know that He can give you the kind of life that, no matter what you've done, lets you begin again. A whole new life.

◆ ◆ ◆

INSIGHT FOR US ALL

Today, Jimmy Lilley is the Director of the Teen Challenge Men's Center in Brockton, Massachusetts. He's played an active part in Teen Challenge for over twenty-eight years. He divides his time between the organization's regional offices located in the center in Brockton, Massachusetts, and his home in New York. There's a lot in Jimmy's story that can speak to every one of us—to people who are using drugs, and even to those of us who are not.

What Jimmy's experience has to say to drug users is this: You think you can stay in control of the drug you're using, but you can't. As Barry McCaffrey, the former U.S. drug czar, has pointed out, the chemicals in drugs actually alter your mind so that your thinking is no longer clear. Any line you set inside yourself as a means of control *will* keep moving until you find yourself doing things and in a shape you never ever planned on. Drugs will erode your will, and erode *you* as a human being.

You can keep denying this if you like. But if you're a drug user, I want to challenge you right now—take an honest look at your life. Have you ever set a limit for yourself and your drug use? Do any of the following promises sound familiar?

"I'll only do light drugs, like pot."

"I'll only do drugs on weekends."

"I'll never go to parties or other places where people are using harder drugs."

"If I go someplace and people are using harder drugs, I'll leave right away."

"I'll only do drugs if someone else buys them or offers them to me."

"I'll never do drugs when my younger siblings or other kids are around."

"I'll never drive, go to work, or go to school while I'm high."

"This was the last time."

Most importantly—did you *keep* that promise? Or did you come up with some kind of reasoning that allowed you to cross that line and move your limit? Sure, all human beings do that in one way or another. It's just that moving the line and pushing limits when it comes to drug use has severe, even deadly, consequences.

There is only one way to rebuild the human spirit when it's been worn down by drug use: Admit that you are unable to stop yourself or even to help yourself. Reach out to a source of help that's greater than you and can't fail. Call upon God. This is where Jimmy's story speaks to every one of us.

We all need the new life that God offers us. It's available, for free, to every one of us who turns to Him and admits that, on our own, we're powerless. In fact, without Him, we're essentially dead, because the human life we're living isn't going to last, is it? God can and will do for any one of us what He did for Jimmy Lilley. The Bible tells us:

> To all who receive him, to those who believe in his name, he gives the right to become children of the living God... children born of God. (JOHN 1:12)

What we are asked to do is to humble ourselves before God, and ask Him to forgive our sins and send His Holy Spirit to live inside of us. This He will do, because His Son Jesus Christ has died to take away all our sin and guilt. Everyone who opens himself to God and experiences this new birth will become a "new creation" in Christ (2 Corinthians 5:17).

Jimmy Lilley spent a lot of years and went down many dead ends looking for something he could count on. He found it in a little church, and in Teen Challenge. What his story teaches us is that when everything in this world fails us, there *is* something we can all count on.

We can count on God's forgiveness and acceptance. We can count on the solid fact that His spirit will give us new life from within to fill our deepest inner longings. If you are involved in drug use, and even if you are not, ask God today for the new life only He can give you. Isn't this what you want?

CHAPTER TWO

"Something Beautiful"

— Lynn Hart —

Today there's an intense focus on the problems faced by kids from troubled and broken homes. Rightly so. The story told in the previous chapter surely supports the claims of experts that kids who have unstable home lives seem to be more at risk for becoming involved in substance abuse and crime.

But the fact is, you don't have to be from that background we hear so much about—the "dysfunctional family"—to get hooked on drugs. You can be from the so-called cream of society, or just from a family that works pretty well, and still get into drugs. It's not necessarily *the motivation* that drove you to take drugs in the first place, but the drugs themselves that can lead you in until you're way over your head. Too many people get into drugs for "recreational" use—and find they're like the swimmer who went for a fun dip in the ocean and found himself caught in a powerful and deadly rip tide.

The question is, how do you begin to find your way back out? That's the position Lynn Hart found herself in, and the question she found herself asking. The answer she discovered can help you if you're caught in the grip of substance abuse—and it also speaks to every one of us who ever needed help with a problem that was too big and overwhelming to handle on our own.

MEET LYNN HART

If you looked at my family from the outside you would have seen, from all appearances, the kind of clean and nicely ordered brood that characterized the 1950s and early 1960s. I was born in Atlanta, the third of five children, into an upper middle-class life. My father was a highly successful businessman—a charming, motivated insurance salesman who made it into the million-dollar round table.

Sometimes they threw big parties, and though the alcohol flowed, they weren't drunken affairs by any stretch. I remember once seeing one of Dad's business associates getting "a little tipsy," but was amazed at the quiet dignity he maintained. If anything, the more alcohol this man consumed, the more he held his head up in an almost regal way, and the more genteel his mannerisms became. After all, Mom and Dad, as well as their friends, were well-heeled, and dedicated church people besides. Our kind of people were never "drunks." Every Sunday, we kids were all scrubbed, dressed, and sitting quietly in our chairs in Sunday school in our suburban Methodist church, surrounded by kids from other "good, southern families." My dad even taught Sunday School.

Our private home life was good, too. I grew up with hugs, kisses, support, and affirmations. We all knew our parents loved us very much, and they seemed to love each other. And there was stability. A time for chores, homework, family fun. There was training in manners—including those famous southern manners, such as the grace that turns its head when someone else has embarrassed themselves, instead of loudly pointing it out and making a show of correcting it. In our home, there was everything necessary to rear children "the right way."

This love and support, and the structure, truly helped me excel. Through grade school and junior high I was an all-A student, and I had a lot of friends. I got along great with my parents and teachers. Because of that, my two older sisters, Anne and Jane, sometimes teased me, calling me "spoiled" and a "goody-goody." But I got along with them well, so I brushed it off. Besides, my parents always wanted the best for me, so it was easy to conform and do what they asked.

No doubt about it, my family liked to present to the world that we were A-Okay. There was just something beautiful about the McMullan clan.

There *was* one little problem. Sometimes my parents fought. It could get pretty physical. There was even a really unhappy time, when I was twelve, when they announced they were getting a divorce. Dad even moved out, more than once, and then came back.

But as quickly as the fights blew up, they disappeared. Suddenly, the atmosphere would go all sunny. The unhappiness, the real issue, just evaporated. I learned in this subtle way that it was important to present an image to the world that we were "just fine, thank you." We were definitely of the southern culture. As long as we were looking fine on the outside, everything *was* fine. I knew there were a lot of people all around me who weren't so fortunate.

Like the dirty men who showed up on Atlanta street corners, bumming change. Or the kids who lived in housing projects—many of whom were being raised by a mom who worked two jobs, or by a grandmother who was trying to get by on public assistance. There were other people, who lived much closer to my world, who were not so fortunate either. The kids who were unpopular, not bright, or troubled loners. Or the kids who just didn't have "the look" that makes you popular. The unlovely kids, or the kids whose families couldn't buy them the right kind of clothes that said you were cool.

We were not *those* people. And so, as I went through grade school in the mid- to late-1960s, and the whole youth culture emerged—and with it, the rough, wild, drug subculture—the life of drug addicts and "dope fiends" was distant and completely foreign to me. In school, in fifth grade, when they began to show us pictures of ugly drugged-out people with runny eyes, long greasy hair, scarred arms, I shuddered and felt disgusted. Looking at these people, I thought, *no way.*

It wasn't that I looked down on people in other classes, or who didn't have what I had. If I thought about them at all, I suppose I felt a mild sense of pity. I certainly couldn't identify with them. Mostly, to be honest, they weren't on my radar screen much at all. My upper-class Atlanta society world was not their world. And their world was just not mine. I didn't know how to relate at all.

And so my world and my life existed with a smooth, somewhat calm surface—a genteel veneer.

In no way were we ready for the turmoil and sadness that was soon to disturb our lives.

The Veneer Cracks

My "nice" life continued as I began junior high. I was still doing well at academics, and I'd gotten into sports. I loved basketball and did well enough to make it onto the school teams.

And then, things began to change. For whatever reason, my sister Jane, who was one year older, started to rebel. At first, there were just tussles with my mom about clothes and hair and makeup. Pretty ordinary stuff. But I could tell something in her attitude was changing, too. We still got along, and I still loved her, but the new Jane scared me a little.

Bit by bit, I pieced together the reason for the attitude change. Or at least where the change had led not only Jane but my oldest sister, Anne, as well. Overhearing a secret phone call here, catching a rumor in school there, I found out Anne had become quite the party girl. She'd been drinking beer with her older friends for some time. Then came the big shocker. At that time—which was the early 1970s—pot was becoming a big thing in our high school. Jane and her friends, I learned, liked to smoke grass.

You'd think that with our upbringing, plus all the anti-drug and anti-drinking alarms educators were setting off, no one would ever touch drugs or alcohol. You'd think we would have had an armored, drug- and alcohol-proofing to keep us well away from such behavior. In a way, though, it seems that in trying to make a point, the schools overdid it. We were told that once you did drugs you were "hooked," and on the fast track to becoming an addict. They emphasized that drugs ruined your mind, made you slow and lethargic, deadened your responses so they killed your athletic abilities, *and*—they added, with a calculated innocence—even deadened your sex drive.

When I first learned what my sisters were into, I was a little upset. We hadn't been brought up to do these kinds of things. What were they thinking?

But by now I was fifteen, and going into my sophomore year. I knew a number of kids in our high school were into drugs. Some were the loners, or the hippie dropout types. But others were good students and athletes. They didn't fit the profile I'd been given of the drug user—that is, someone whose life fell apart overnight, leaving them a hopelessly messed-up addict, dirty and eating out of dumpsters, picking up diseases from shared needles.

In a way—but not to fault the school's efforts—I think they may have gone a little overboard in presenting the horrors of drugs to us. Another way to say it is, if they thought scaring kids away from drugs would work, it didn't. For one thing, a lot of kids don't scare very easily. In fact, if something's risky, or scary, or edgy, they run to it. And then there was the fact that some of the kids who used drugs were actually good students and athletes. In their experience, some drugs could mellow you out, and others could sharpen your mind and make you more alert. Certain drugs could crank your energy levels way up and give you the competitive edge in sports.

And then, of course, there was the influence of the popular music culture. Pretty much, the message was: *Your mother and your teacher—they aren't going to tell you the truth about drugs. But we will. The cool people and the tuned-in people are all using.*

I suppose the bottom line for me was this: I began to put two and two together and realize that drinking and drugs were not as terrible as all the warnings made them out to be. And a lot of good kids all around me—including, I now knew, my two older sisters—seemed to be having one heck of a good time using alcohol and drugs. They were having a blast, in fact, and they were holding it together. Despite what the "anti" people said, I began to see beneath their fear-laden messages. They wanted to control kids. From what I could see, the reality of what happened to people who drank and used drugs was different than what they'd told us. And so the arguments for avoiding these substances cracked and fell apart in my head.

One afternoon, just after school began, I found Jane alone in her room. Mom must have been out somewhere and Dad was working. The place was pretty quiet. She was laying on her bed listening to music, and rolled over as I walked in.

"So I hear you've got a crush on Brent," she said, half-teasing.

Brent was a *very* nice-looking guy I'd met. "Yeah," I said. "Actually, I like him a lot."

She nodded approvingly. That's one thing that bound Jane and me together. I knew some friends whose older sisters tried to play mom with them. They hated it, and I would have, too. Jane never tried to pull that with me. If anything, she got a glint in her eye when I did something that remotely pushed the edge.

"So," she said, smiling, "I'm kind of wondering…"

"Wondering *what?*" I asked.

She rolled off the mattress, went to her closet, and fished around behind her clothes. In a moment she returned and sat beside me on the bed, holding a joint. "I was wondering if you'd wanna try smoking one these."

I didn't even hesitate. I took it between my fingers. "Sure. Why not?"

What followed that single incident was, in fact, a kind of a revolution. Once my surface resistance to the rebellious stuff my sisters were doing cracked, I dropped in nicely to the world of partying, drinking, and drugs. Just like that. And I felt pretty daring and sophisticated.

We began having parties at the house when my parents were away. I also began double dating with Jane and her boyfriend and with Brent. Brent was another reason for the rapid change I underwent in the fall of my sophomore year. Brent was definitely *not* from the Atlanta social stratum my parents would have approved. He was kind of rough and I just knew my parents wouldn't like him. Seeing him without my parents' knowledge made it more exciting, and it also gave me that rebel mystique. Probably, it also stirred some adolescent sense of high drama, in that we were like "star-crossed lovers," concealing our love from my parents who would undoubtedly want to thwart us.

When my parents first found out about Brent, it wasn't pleasant.

"Lynn, come in here," my father said one day, summoning me to the family room. Mom was sitting on the sofa, and my brother and sisters were nowhere around. I sensed something was up.

"We're aware that you aren't just going out to the movies with Jane and her boyfriend and 'some friends of theirs' like you've been telling us," Dad plunged right in. "We know you're dating a young man named Brent who's pretty wild." He might as well have said, "…who carries a machine gun."

I looked from Dad to Mom. Both of them looked pretty stern. It wouldn't do any good to lie. "Well, we started out as just friends," I replied, lamely. "But yeah, we like each other now and… "

Dad cut in. "Your mother and I do not want you to date him. He may be a good person, I don't know. You seem to have kept him hidden from us." As he said this, I could tell Dad was doing a good job of controlling his unhappiness with me. For her part, Mom was nodding in agreement with him and looking every bit as displeased.

"He's really a good guy," I protested. But I didn't get far.

"Let me say it plainly, Lynn," Dad went on firmly. "You are not to go out with this young man. From what I hear about him, he's not good boyfriend material for you."

For a second, I wondered how he'd learned about Brent. But more than that, I got the message under his words. *He's not from our class of people.* Not that Dad was some kind of southern bigot. I'm sure he was like any other father who's ever raised his children with high standards and tried to give them the best life possible. But his authoritarian approach, together with this subtly superior attitude, was like throwing a match on gasoline.

I knew a frontal assault wasn't going to work. So I just stared back at him, giving no indication of what I was thinking as my mind worked quickly.

For one thing, he hadn't exactly said I was forbidden to see Brent. And for another thing, I could use that veneer of southern agreeableness for my own purposes if I had to. I had no intention whatsoever of *not* seeing Brent whenever I darn well pleased.

Calmly, dodging the issue, I said, "He's just a friend. You don't have to worry."

If Daddy thought for a second he'd nipped a problem in the bud, he had some shocking surprises in store.

I kept right on dating Brent. The fact that Mom and Dad didn't like him made my feelings for him more intense. To go undetected, I'd tell my parents I was going to a friend's house and that I might stay late watching a movie on TV. Then I'd truck right off to meet Brent. I don't remember considering for even one second how badly I was misusing and betraying their trust. In fact, we were becoming more involved physically, quickly moving beyond kissing and making out.

Brent was introducing me to more than sex, too. If Dad had known Brent was dealing drugs he would have locked me in my room. We still did pot, but it was light fare now. Brent taught me how to experiment with mixing different harder drugs. I loved him, and wanted to act sophisticated enough around him to fit in with his older crowd. I also wanted to be like my older sisters, who were definitely over the top now. And I liked stepping apart from the herd of nice, dull kids. "Nice" had gotten real old.

As a result, by the second half of my sophomore year, I'd moved out of the more popular sports-and-academics crowd and moved into the "bad girls" crowd.

Daddy never seemed to suspect—until the bombshell went off.

I got pregnant. Overwhelmed, the only solution my parents could think of was to take me to New York, where abortion had recently been legalized.

Obviously, after that I was strictly forbidden to see Brent. Period. It did absolutely no good. I would say I'd been asked to baby-sit. I'd say they'd told me they were staying out very, very late so my parents wouldn't expect me home until the wee hours. They discovered my lie, and now it was war.

My solution was to run away. Frantic that their fifteen-year-old daughter might be living out on the streets—or worse, living with her lover—my parents tried desperately to find me. I avoided them and all the conflict that would come with facing them. I also began staying out of school to be with Brent, and of course my grades dropped like a rock.

Partway through my junior year, my truancy and my grades had gotten so bad, the school was ready to kick me out. I got my head together enough to get myself into another high school, and pulled my grades and my act out of the tailspin.

Though I did manage to pull off some good grades, I really didn't get myself together. In fact, I was getting deeper into drugs. Brent and a girlfriend introduced me to speed. We'd combine hallucinogenics with speed—and off I'd go to school.

This was not like tripping on acid, because I knew I had to maintain appearances at school so I wouldn't be found out and suspended. I was very alert, up—hyper-focused. Every word teachers said was intense. But the euphoria, and the colors running together—it made all the tedious boredom of classes bearable.

Once again, I was keeping it together on the outside. What did I care if I'd earned the reputation as a druggie? I was maintaining. I remembered the man at my parents' party who held his head up with regal bearing even while he was actually dead drunk. I actually felt proud of myself that I could "handle it."

Now it really didn't matter to me what the "nice" kids said about me. One day, about this time, I was getting ready for school, standing in front of a bathroom mirror—when I suddenly became very aware of my reflection. What I saw was a blond girl who was very much alive and okay, a girl who had been named only two years before to the Homecoming Court, an upper-class-looking kid with clean hair, good skin, nice clothes. Sure, I was heavily into drugs. But I was nothing like those ugly, dirty, drug-bums whose pictures they'd shown us all through school.

If anything, I felt *very* together.

REALITY

Somehow I managed to graduate with my class. I was now eighteen, and of course my parents had college plans for me. I suppose they were more desperate than ever to get me on a good track. I didn't want any part of college. Who needed a bunch of professors putting demands on you? What was the point of getting a degree—a piece of paper to hang on your wall—just to show you'd turned yourself into a trained dog for four years and knew how to jump through hoops for a bunch of geeks? That was my attitude.

Jane had moved out and basically declared her independence. She was living with friends in an apartment. They were all doing heroin. Once, I helped her tie her arm and watched her shoot up. What scared me was that I could see she was trapped.

Odd, though. I was getting the picture that all the substances we were running through our bodies were not that good for us. But I didn't seem to care. Or I had no self-control. Or I'd tell myself, *I'll never get that bad.* But I was thrilled to be getting drugs for free from Jane and her friends. And every night I came home to my parents' house drunk or high or both.

My parents managed to talk me into college. Every penny of their money went down the drain. I partied the whole time and only went to class when I felt like it, which wasn't too often. Weekends, I'd sneak home to be with Brent. Sometimes I'd look at my class schedule and intend to get my act together. But there wasn't an ounce of follow-through in me.

Life was one huge party. And my sisters and I were going to live it up.

One Saturday evening, in my second year, I went with some friends to the gym to watch a basketball game. After that, it would be party time. At some point, a friend I was with grabbed my arm and pointed toward the door of the gym. "Wow, something's really wrong with *her*." I looked and saw a girl I knew, a neighbor, hurrying across the floor in front of the bleachers. She seemed frantic, and tears streamed down her face. She shouted something to people up in the bleachers, and they pointed in our direction. She turned and our eyes connected, and she ran to where I was sitting.

"Lynn. *Lynn.*" She came up to me, sobbing, shaking, near hysteria.

"I got a phone call. Your parents are trying to find you… *Your sister Jane is dead.*"

The shock that went through me is indescribable. And so is the numbness I lived in all through the next days and the ordeal of Jane's funeral. Jane was dead at twenty. She'd been high on a mix of heroin and a kind of speed, and suffocated on her own vomit. Her friends had apparently left her.

The devastation I felt was pretty terrible. The night I'd gotten home, I found the minister of our church there. Not knowing what else to do, he'd given mom alcohol to calm her down. But Mom and Dad were caught up in anger at each other, and blame was flying back and forth like punches. Shouts of "I should have divorced you years ago" filled the air. My younger sister was in total chaos, too, because Jane's death wasn't the only turmoil to break over our heads. Earlier that day, before Jane's body had been discovered, my brother, Bob, had been arrested and taken to a juvenile detention home.

How had a good family, from a good neighborhood, with such good intentions about life, wound up here—so broken, utterly devastated, and with no hope?

After Jane's funeral, I would go back to college. There was nothing else to do. But *that* was really pointless. Any pretense of wanting to be there to study was gone. On one hand, I resolved not to let drugs get me. And on the other hand, alcohol and drugs were my big comforts. The reality of my life seemed pretty crummy, empty, and hopeless.

A Look in the Mirror

I didn't know this for some time, but back at home something drastic was happening. Two weeks after Jane's death, a new minister arrived at our church. He learned about our news and paid a visit to my parents. He seemed to have something more to offer Mom than the medication of alcohol.

With compassion, he listened to Mom pour out of her broken heart all the grief over the wreckage that was our family—about a marriage that had run aground, one child dead, three others lost in drugs and alcohol. Then, taking her hand, he looked her in the eye. "Jo, what are you willing to do about it?"

"Anything," she replied.

"Good," he said, with a gentle smile. "I know what will help you."

I also learned later that Dad had not been so sure at first about the minister's answer. In fact, for some months he didn't want anything to do with it.

Mom kept her solution to herself for some time. And caught up in my own world as I was, it took me some time to notice the slow but really big change that was coming over her. And then, maybe three or four months after Jane's death, I noticed a good change in Dad, too. Oddly enough, I felt something good must be happening at home, even though my parents had recently informed me I could visit, but couldn't return to live under their roof as long as I was drinking and doing drugs. Since the college had seen no future in me, I'd moved into an apartment in a crummy part of Atlanta with friends.

One Saturday, I dropped in on Mom. I'd become really curious. "So," I asked, "what's the big change around here all about?"

It came down to this: At the moment Mom had faced the reality that the perfect life she'd tried to build was never going to be—that she could no longer handle the life she had—the new minister had asked, "Are you willing to let God take over?"

So that was it. Mom and Dad had gotten religion.

I listened politely as Mom explained how she and Dad had prayed and asked God to take control of their lives. How they had committed themselves to serving Christ, instead of serving just themselves. As she talked, I added up all the quiet but definite changes I'd seen in my parents.

For one thing, there was this calm, or peace, that showed through even in the moments when there was sadness in their eyes. I'd fully expected them to announce they were divorcing, but something pretty fantastic had to have happened to given them the peace I sensed in them and to bring them together more closely than I'd ever witnessed. I'd seen them as a team before—but now they were more willing to talk things out rather than fight them out.

In Mom, the change was probably a little more pronounced. She'd put on music, and go around cooking and cleaning. It wasn't that she was ignoring Jane's death or Bob's arrest. In fact, she seemed to have a strength and peace to talk about these things without falling apart. From that evidence alone, I had to believe something—maybe it was God—had changed her.

But this God stuff. It was not for me. In my mind, Jane had let her partying get out of control. I wouldn't do that. And I sure wasn't ready to give up my fun. As I got ready to go back to school after that weekend, I realized there was one other big change I'd witnessed. For years, nearly every conversation with Mom and Dad had been strained. With Mom I always felt a pressure coming from her where my lifestyle was concerned. There was always some disapproving comment made about my wild behavior, my poor grades, my attitude, or how much unhappiness I was causing. This weekend—and for some weeks, actually—there was none of that.

"I'm praying for you," was all Mom said as I walked out the door. For *sure*, I thought, something big had happened to change that lady!

No, I didn't want religion. But compared to Mom's new demeanor, which only became more peaceful in the coming months, I could see that I was becoming a mess. The change in her, and Dad too, was like a mirror that really showed me how bad I was doing. Time was passing. I was well out of high school now and pushing twenty-two and I had absolutely nothing to show for my life.

What Mom didn't know—what I was hiding even from friends—was the fact that I'd begun to sell my blood to get money for alcohol. Things didn't work out with the apartment, and I wound up bouncing around to different friends' homes. Now I stayed loaded all the time. If I wasn't drinking, I was smoking pot. If I wasn't doing one or the other, I was miserable.

And still…

Still I managed to keep up a great front that I was holding it all together. In my head I was still the healthy, athletic basketball player who made the Homecoming Court and had a lot of potential—even though that reality had played itself out. Around my friends I'd talk big-talk about what I was going to do with my life. The fact that my plans and dreams changed, and I did nothing at all to achieve them, gave me no clue as to how totally unstable and lost in dreams I was.

I even managed to keep up a professional demeanor at the florist's job I'd landed. I prided myself on having enough sophistication to hold it together at work—even though I'd spend my lunch hours drinking and return to the shop drunk.

Then, in short order, it all fell apart.

Brent and I had been together for six years. He was more into drugs now than ever. When—big surprise—my job at the florist didn't work out, I moved into his house. I realized that I couldn't even hold a job. And so I started doing coke. I'd get really up... but then I'd come down and that was terrible. To cover the bad feeling, I'd drink.

It was at that point, one morning, that a terrible truth hit me.

I woke to an empty house. Brent had gone to work. I got up to go into the bathroom, my stomach churning with nausea in the aftermath of the coke I'd snorted last night. When I got there, I was in a cold sweat and had to lay my head on the cool porcelain of the sink. I wished Brent were here. He was never here. He was always out and we spent no time together.

Barely able to pick my head up, I looked at my reflection in the mirror. My skin was gray, my eyes were red, and my hair hung limp around my face. At the same moment, the thought hit me. *If you were Brent, would you want to be around you?*

If I hadn't felt so strung-out and numb inside, I might have cried. Truth hit home and hit hard. I'd been so practiced at holding the surface of my life together. Or at least telling myself I was. But I'd lost everything: my high school years, my chance at college and a future, my sister, and now, I knew, my boyfriend. But that wasn't even the worst of it.

I reached one hand up and pressed my fingers against the mirror. It was hot in here and the glass was warm to the touch. The silvered surface was as shallow as I felt.

You are a hollow shell, I thought. *And your life is an empty waste.*

OUT OF THE DARKNESS

I woke up to find myself in pitch-blackness. I could only tell I was lying on a bare mattress in a basement. Vaguely, I remembered getting stoned out of my head and calling someone to drive me from Brent's house. Where? And how long had I been here?

Groping around, I found a stairway and bumped my way noisily to a door at the top of the steps. As I turned the handle, someone pulled the door open—the sight of me causing her to scream. It was Mom. Poor thing. Stepping back, with her hand on her pounding chest, staring wide-eyed at the disheveled thing coming up out of the darkness. Me.

"You nearly scared me to death, Lynn. When did you come home? No one heard you come in," she said in a rush.

I wobbled my way over to the kitchen table and sank down in a chair. "I don't know, Mom," I said. I'd hit bottom, and the tears welled up. "I don't even really know how I got here. I… I need help, Mom."

The look on Mom's face told me those were four of the most wonderful words she'd ever heard. It had been years since she'd begun to pray for me. Before she could say anything, I rushed on.

"Help me find someplace to go. Even if you and Dad won't pay for it, I'll work out something on my own."

Mom was watching at me with a sort of disbelieving look. I wondered if she was thinking, *I'll believe that when I see it.* Instead, she walked over to the counter, fished through a stack of mail, and returned to plunk an envelope down on the table in front of me.

"You're not going to believe this, Lynn, but God has already found a place for you to go for help."

Just five days before, she told me, a mass-mailing piece had arrived in the mail—from a Christian ministry for young women needing to come off drugs. Mom knew I'd already met someone who was involved in a ministry like this, called Teen Challenge, but I'd blown them off. But for some reason, she felt moved inside to fast and pray for me that I'd come to the end of the line and wake up to my need. She'd fasted for three days and, just that morning, milling about the kitchen, felt she was getting a message in the quiet of her heart:

You can stop fasting. Your prayers for Lynn have been answered.

"And so here I was," she said, beaming through her own tears, "feeling like maybe the war was finally over. And a few minutes later I hear someone dragging up the basement stairs. I don't mean to sound so faithless, but it's hard to believe this is happening."

When Mom put her arms around me, I crumbled completely. We sobbed and sobbed together. I wanted to believe she was right—that I was ready to come out of the dark about the serious mess I was in, and that the war was finally over.

Finding Out What It Takes

I got a ticket and flew up to New York, to the girls' home Mom had read about in the mailer. This was part of the Teen Challenge ministry, a place called the Walter Hoving Home.

I made fast progress. The Bentons, who directed the program, were like spiritual parents to all of us girls, and they spent hours answering my many questions. Besides that, I'd come with an attitude that I would do whatever it took to get free from my addictions. Why not? I'd lived my life my own way and look where it got me.

Quickly, I learned how to blend with people from all different backgrounds, not just my upper-class circles. It wasn't that I was a snob. I'd just never had to get out of my own cultural niche and learn to listen to people who were not like me and learn about their lives. From girls who lived in ghettos and on the streets as hookers—man, did I get some new perspectives on life!

I also learned how to socialize without drugs and alcohol. I had honestly never known how to do that.

In small group sessions, and just in living together, we were also trained in how to handle our squabbles and disagreements. In many ways, every one of us came into the program at what was probably the emotional level of an eight- or ten-year-old. Anger and fights could erupt over the pettiest things. The counselors taught us how to calm things down, talk it out, and negotiate a good solution.

There was also Bible study, prayer, and worship. Like Mom and

Dad, I too had prayed and asked Jesus Christ to come into my life. Never, in all the years I'd attended our Atlanta mainline church, had anyone ever told me you can enter into the kind of personal, daily relationship with the God the Bible speaks of. The study leaders and counselors filled in many of the gaping holes in my spiritual knowledge—about prayer, serving God, loving others, and what the Christian life was all about.

Weeks ran into months, and I began to be able to stand in front of a mirror and look at myself squarely in the face for the first time in a long while. I could hardly believe it, but I was getting it together again.

One of the truly big and remarkable changes that surprised me was the fact that I had become very disciplined.

The Home was very goal oriented. After the first six weeks, during which you basically got clean, you could start to qualify for certain jobs. After three months, you could become a "big sister" and show incoming girls the ropes and watch out for them. At six months, you could join the choir. I liked this system. After using my talents for lying, betraying, covering up, and drug dealing, it was good to finally feel like I was using my abilities in productive ways. And after bombing out at life, I now had the sense I was doing something with myself, progressing, and going someplace.

HOME STRETCH

Not everyone was happy with the tightly run schedule the Home kept us on, but I turned on to it. I'd get up early. Do my chores. Go to studies or small group sessions. And in my free time I'd exercise. A nice glow had returned to my skin. My muscles were toning up. Instead of hanging limp, my hair had a healthy luster again.

One afternoon, I finished my exercise program and went out for my run. I was feeling great and wanted to push myself.

When I came back to the "home stretch," right in front of the Home, I kicked it extra hard, sprinting right through the finish. I walked it off and, as I went inside to get a shower, a new girl stopped me and commented on how disciplined I was at exercising. Feeling pretty good about myself, I thanked her and told her I planned to work at it harder, and that she should try running or at least walking for exercise.

As I turned for my room, my big sister stopped me. "What was that all about?"

"What was *what* about?"

"That girl is right off the streets, where she was eating out of dumpsters. She needs to get healthy...and she sure doesn't need to be encouraged to leave this place and go out for walks."

"Look, I didn't mean anything by it. I was just trying to be friendly," I said, feeling a little irritated with her. Where did she get off, jumping on me like this? All I wanted was to go shower.

"You know," she went on, "I need to be honest with you about this exercise program of yours."

Suddenly, I was all ears.

She folded her arms across her chest, and suddenly I got the full dress-down. It seemed to her I might be trying to impress someone. Or maybe I was working out to attract special attention to myself. Was that it—was I trying to impress the people who ran the program? Did I think maybe I'd get a better leadership role over the other girls if I looked like I was super-disciplined?

Now to be totally honest, those were not her exact words—but I interpreted her words and believed she thought I was a total fake.

By the time she was through and I'd stormed upstairs to hit the shower, I was furious. Was that what everyone here thought of me—that I was just a phony? I let the hot water stream over me as I clenched my teeth, thinking, *I hate her. And I hate this place.* The minute I was dry, I was going to throw my clothes in a suitcase and just leave.

I don't need this. I can leave this behind in a heartbeat and it won't matter one bit.

Even as my angry thoughts boiled inside, it was as if a little light came on. It was as if someone took me by the shoulders, and made me step back to take a good look at myself. Right in the middle of my tirade, a new thought came: *This is what you've done all your life, Lynn. It's your pattern. On the outside, you can work hard and achieve whatever you put your mind to—you're strong and you can stick with it. But inside, whenever something makes you uncomfortable, you immediately want to run away.*

All the fire went out of me. I strongly suspected this was God talking to me, because—even though I hated to hear it—it was the dead-honest truth about who I was. That's the moment I found out what it was going to take for me to become a spiritually healthy and maturing person.

First, I had to stop running away from things that made me uncomfortable. Running away to avoid discomfort hadn't gotten me into drugs, but it had become part and parcel of my life the deeper I'd gotten into them. I didn't want to run away any more. I wanted to have the strength and courage to face problems and work them through.

Second, if I *really* wanted to learn healthy discipline for my life, I'd started at the wrong place—with the outside, and disciplining my body. What I needed to learn was how to discipline my spirit. How to direct my own thoughts and make my own choices instead of reacting to people, like my big sister. And most especially how to control my emotions and not let my life be directed by how I felt. Boy, had *that* ever gotten me in big trouble.

Suddenly, I could see that changing these ways of responding would be, for me, the *real* home stretch.

I did not pack my things. I stayed. Even though my big sister had been dead wrong about my motives for getting in shape, I would not let my little wounded feelings cause me to run. And from that day, my life really took off in a new direction.

The next time I saw my big sister, I calmly, confidently spoke up for myself. I did not cop an attitude. I just told her what I was trying to do for myself, and asked her to trust me when I said I had no hidden motives. Without making an issue, I also told her that, honestly, her words had hurt me, but that I didn't want to let hard feelings come between us. Could we forgive each other and move on? Whatever had been going on in her head before, she asked my forgiveness now for judging me.

Later, alone in my room, I was grateful for the new relationship with God. I truly believed it was His light that showed me my unhealthy pattern of behavior, and His voice that told me what to do to change it. A tiny incident that could have been the undoing of all my progress had become a major turning point, and spiritual growth, for me.

Somehow I knew I'd turned a really big corner. There was a song we sang, and I came to think of it as a song that spoke about my life, and maybe the lives of many young women I'd met. It was about God and the way He'd changed our lives. Some of the words were:

"All I had to offer Him was brokenness and strife, but He made something beautiful of my life."

As a kid, my family had projected an outer image that we were the successful American family. The "beautiful" people, so to speak. But without any spiritual foundation at all, all the ugliness and strife of our many human failings had nearly destroyed us. Amazingly, God had taken what we'd offered Him even if it amounted to broken pieces. He wasn't finished with me yet, or with my family, by any means.

But I knew He was going to make of my life something new and beautiful.

◆ ◆ ◆

Insight for Us All

Lynn's story is an amazing testimony to the way God is at work around us, trying to make Himself known to us. As for Lynn herself, she went on to a special counselor-training camp run by the founder of Teen Challenge, David Wilkerson. There, among other things, she met her husband, Rodney Hart, who tells his own story later in this book. Today, Lynn teaches and trains the ladies at the Teen Challenge Women's Center in Providence, Rhode Island.

Lynn's story also has a lot to teach us.

First, on a very practical note, the educators in Lynn's school, and probably many others, oversold the dangers of certain drugs. When Lynn and her friends heard from other kids that the school's information wasn't accurate, they went with what they learned from friends. The authority of their friends' experience outstripped the authority of teachers and parents.

When we give information about substances and their effects, we need to be accurate. Scare tactics will not work. Information alone will not build personal walls against the onslaught of the substances that flow freely in our society.

More important than giving out information is the work of helping people build healthy spiritual lives.

Second, on the spiritual side, probably every one of us wears some sort of mask, or keeps up some appearance for the sake of looking good in the eyes of other people. Maybe we like to have people see us as strong and independent, "self made." Maybe we want to be seen as different, special. Some people even like the outcast look.

Underneath all our masks, though, we are largely the same. We don't like to face hurt, discomfort, disappointment, or pain. And we sure don't like to be honest about our own failings. The one key difference, however, seems to be the way we attempt to escape those feelings and cover our failings when confronted with them.

Keeping up a front didn't work for Lynn or her family. But we don't have to become lost in a drug haze, like Lynn, before we learn how to humble ourselves and admit that other people have better answers—or that they have their lives together in ways we don't. Humility, admitting we need help, is *the* major step every one of us needs to make if we're going to find help from beyond ourselves. Especially God's help.

Are you willing to face the fact that you need God and His help? And that you may need the help of others in some area of your life? Or maybe with your entire life?

In the final analysis, it doesn't matter how well or how long we've "held it together" on the outside. It makes no difference how good our mask looks to other people. If we have no spiritual depth and strength on the inside, we're wide open to failure—and sitting ducks for influences like drugs, alcohol, workaholism, sexual addiction, and other escapes.

Third, when we refuse to reach out for help from beyond ourselves, from God or anyone else, we doom ourselves to trying over and over the same solutions that never worked for us before.

For the substance abuser, this means repeating the same patterns of thinking and feeling, the way Lynn did. The result is that she dug a deep rut in her life, going over and over the same ground—and all the while she wondered why she seemed to be getting nowhere.

But there's something more going on than just the insanity of doing the same thing, getting the same unhappy result, and doing it again. If you take a close look, you'll see there's a fair amount of just plain stubbornness involved in the unhealthy things we do over and over again.

Stubbornness—resistance to hearing someone else's idea of how we should live—seems to be a special problem for us human beings. It's especially a problem for people caught up in addictions. They're willing to reject what experts—people who have studied the effects of, say, alcohol or drugs—have to say about their dangerous, damaging, and long-term effects. The sad thing is, too many find they have stubbornly chosen their own way only to find out too late they were wrong. Some, like Lynn's sister Jane, have been dead wrong.

Teen Challenge, and programs like the one Lynn attended, helps reestablish a healthy relationship with the authorities we all need in life. Whether it's in school, on the job, or in the community, life just works better for us when we have healthy respect for authority and know how to interact in a responsible, mature way with those who are appointed or elected or hired to be over us. One secret of Teen Challenge's success is that it helps people learn how to submit to loving, Christian authority. Most who are in the program discover that this is one of the healthiest things they can do to restore sanity, stability, and order to their personal lives.

How about you? Whether you are involved in drug and alcohol abuse or not, have you submitted your life to an authority beyond yourself? Or are you still making up your own rules as you go along? And if you are—*honestly* now—how's it going? Have you found out yet that there's more struggle and stress in this than it's worth?

Today, ask God to help you lay aside any masks you've been wearing. He sees you the way you really are already, and He is willing to take you just the way you are. You don't need to keep up a front with Him. You will find out what a relief it is when you stop trying to live up to any image, and instead become authentically the person He made you to be.

Ask God, too, to help you lay aside any pride that may be keeping you from asking for help in any area of your life—whether it's with your marriage or family, your finances and your career, or with drugs, alcohol, or other addictions.

If you do, you will be amazed at the power and the wisdom He brings to help you. Try it. Right now.

CHAPTER THREE

"NO CHANCE ON EARTH"

— Floyd Miles —

Lynn's story—good kid, from a good family, gets hooked on drugs—isn't surprising anymore, is it? We know that people from all walks of life are using heavily and becoming addicts. What with the ready availability of drugs, even at the grade school level, more people are getting hooked every day.

What's surprising, given the fact that drugs seriously alter brain chemistry, is that people who come to Teen Challenge are getting off drugs. With a success rate of *80 percent*, who can argue that Teen Challenge doesn't offer the right answer to addiction? Teen Challenge's success extends even to people who—given their background, and from all outward appearances—seem to have no chance but to live out their days as nothing but an addict.

Floyd Miles was one of those people. Floyd was a kid from the mean streets of Harlem, who seemed destined from childhood to end his days in the gutter. What happened to him on his way to what seemed to be a very bad end is nothing less than a miracle.

◆ ◆ ◆

MEET FLOYD MILES

I was playing in the elementary school yard with my grade school friends, when one of them nudged me. "That man outside the fence. He's staring at you, Floyd."

Turning, I looked at the rusted chain-link barrier that surrounded our play area, protecting us from the rough people that always roamed the Harlem streets. Sure enough, the man at the fence was staring right at me. His clothes were wrinkled and dirty; his face and hands were covered with abscesses and sores.

My heart leaped, and I ran toward the fence.

But when he saw me coming, the man turned and ran off down the sidewalk.

"Daddy!" I shouted after him when I reached the fence. "Daddy, come back!" But he hustled across the street, barely dodging a taxi, and disappeared around a corner into the jungle of concrete surrounding us.

My fingers gripped the chain links, as hot tears came to my eyes.

"Hey, Floyd," my friends called. But I couldn't turn and let them see me crying like a little baby. I just gripped the fence as my heart tried to race after the daddy who couldn't even look me in the face or talk to me. He was on one of his binges.

Right at that moment, this rusted fence was one of the few solid things I could hold onto in my whole life.

NO ONE TO COUNT ON

When I was six, I'd experienced a real trauma.

It was a warm day. Mom, Grandma, and Mom's sister had decided we should head out of the city and picnic somewhere along the Hudson River. But as we were getting ready to leave, Mom said she wasn't feeling well. We left her lying on the couch, resting.

The burgers were cooking on the grill, and I was throwing stones in the river, when Mom's boyfriend suddenly pulled up in a taxi. "You've got to come home," he told Grandma. "Something's wrong."

It was all chaos, packing up and driving back to the apartment. But when we got there, Mom was gone. They said it was a heart attack. She was just twenty-eight.

I was left with Grandma, and with my aunt and my two cousins.

So there we were, struggling to make a life for ourselves in a small flat.

Myself, I thought Grandma was pretty much a saint. She was the hardest working lady I knew. Grandma came limping up the stairs after work, with her old legs throbbing because she'd been on her feet for ten solid hours. She was exhausted. Though my aunt disciplined us, we actually got away with a lot.

Sometimes I'd get blurred memories of my mom. I remembered her going out to get milk and not coming home for two weeks. The funny and not-so-funny thing was, when she did come home she always had the milk.

All this to say, yes, I had a roof over my head and food to eat and a praying Grandma who loved me. My two cousins were as close to a brother and sister as I would get. My real sister and I were split up because Grandma couldn't take us both in. My sister lived with my great-aunt. But from the earliest I can remember, I had this deep, deep sense that I was pretty much on my own. It was like a big empty feeling inside.

Once in a while Dad would show up suddenly. It set Grandma's teeth on edge, I knew, but she'd allow him to take me to visit his side of the family. We'd make our rounds and they'd give me money. On the sidewalk outside Grandma's apartment, he'd stop me.

"How about you give your old man that money." I'd fish all the bills out of my pocket and put them in his hand. I knew it would go to buy heroin. Even so, I just couldn't hate him. In spite of it all, I really loved him.

That's the way life was. I didn't know any different. Still, what chance on earth did a kid like me have of making it?

A Kid With "Promise"

Things being what they were at home, I'd have to say I got my education on the streets. When I was about eleven, I started working at odd jobs—sweeping up a barbershop, stocking shelves in a grocery store, working in record shop. Somehow there was always an older person who at least pointed out what I needed to do and helped keep me out of trouble.

At fifteen or sixteen, I began working in a pool hall. The owner sold drugs, and I worked for his partner, helping in his numbers racket. Oddly enough, both of these guys had a heart of gold toward me and the other kids who hung out there. "I want you guys to stay out of trouble," he'd say, smiling, "or I'll box your head." Because of him, I stayed away from the bad stuff and made money, while most of the kids I'd known since grade school were now doing kid stuff.

Earlier, the Harlem school system had identified me and some other kids as having "promise." A bunch of us were transferred to a school for the intelligent and gifted.

The evening Grandma and I took the city bus to my new school for orientation I was excited. What would it be like to be in a new school, with better equipment, and with kids of different races? It felt like a whole new world opening up for me. Someone thought I had *promise* and that I was *gifted.*

All the other kids' parents were eager, alert, asking questions. And right in the middle of it all, Grandma—poor, tired lady—fell sound asleep. Everyone around us could hear her loud breathing, and I died of embarrassment. What was a kid from the tenements doing here?

Two Roads

In 1973, my aunt died. She had tried to raise me the best way she could. So now the little bit of discipline I'd had was gone. My aunt had been a heavy drinker for years. Her blood pressure had always run high, and drinking didn't help her cause one bit.

Now Grandma was left to raise us three kids on her own. To put it that way, though, is a joke. With everything resting on her shoulders, all she could do, literally, was work to keep body and soul together. The laundry consumed long daytime shifts. And church was the only comfort and encouragement for the soul of a sweet, sweet woman who had outlived her own daughters. Beyond that, we really were on our own.

Now, more and more, the streets were becoming my home.

One morning in math class, as I sat listening to the most boring lecture about hypotenuses something-squared, the thought occurred to me, *what am I doing here?*

For one thing, living in the ghetto—well, it was a whole different world from this school and these teachers with their rosy outlook on life. Our tenement building was getting dirtier and more decrepit with every passing year, nothing like this well-lit, freshly painted school with its shiny polished floors. And all this talk about working for a career—the people in my neighborhood were all service-class, grinding it out in tough, dirty jobs. These teachers were talking about a different world from the one I went back to when I walked out these doors.

What am I doing here? That, and other new thoughts, started occurring. Say I didn't show up in class and the school phoned to check on me—no one was even home now to take the call. Say I needed money. Between working the numbers and other fast-buck jobs, I could quickly slide a few hundred dollars in my pocket any time I wanted. Why did I really *need* an education? Why take the hard road and do all this work when I could make a lot of money a much easier way?

With no adult input to challenge my thinking, I began skipping school. Life hanging out on the streets was great. No one bossed me around, but there were opportunities to make money. People accepted me, so I didn't have to work for the approval good grades had brought me. In fact, I didn't have to work at all. I began partying, drinking, smoking reefer, and sniffing cocaine. Who needed some degree—some piece of paper—to get me where I wanted to go? The street could teach me everything I wanted to know.

In 1975, at seventeen years old, I dropped out of high school. And I became a father. Tia was my beautiful baby girl. The only downer was, I was an irresponsible, drug-using adolescent. No way was I prepared to give this incredible, gorgeous little girl what she needed and deserved in the way of a stable home. If it even crossed my mind that I was condemning my own child to the same childhood-minus-a-healthy-daddy I'd had, I blocked it out.

So instead of choosing the life-road that led through education to a career and stability, I took another road. I'd make my way using street smarts.

It never occurred to me ask myself: How smart—*really*—were these choices I was making?

ANGEL DUST

Shortly after the birth of my daughter, my hustle in the numbers racket was drying up. The guy I'd worked for had lost his credibility.

To make matters worse, a new drug had hit the streets earlier and taken Harlem by storm. *Angel dust*. I'd been experimenting with it from time to time, but it seemed now to be getting out of hand. For one thing, my personality drastically changed. Because of that my daughter's mother and I broke up. I wasn't "Floyd, the nice guy" any more. Things didn't work out, and I moved back to my grandmother's tenement building.

Doing dust was a *real* problem almost from my first puff. In my head, I thought I'd found heaven. I felt light. Strong. Like I could take on the world. I'd never been very athletic—but angel dust gave me amazing strength. I could do a hundred pushups on a bet. Beat anyone in a bike race. I was on top of the world.

That is, if you didn't factor in the downside of my lifestyle. Once, I got out of my head at a party and tried to throw a girl out a window. The next day I didn't even remember it.

And there was the way I was living. Grandma's building had become so gross and run-down that it was condemned. Grandma had moved out, and so had the rest of my family—with the exception of one cousin, another addict, who was also living in the decrepit apartment. The building that had once housed my family was quickly becoming a haven for druggies and other down-and-outers.

I told myself I was just temporarily "down on my luck." I refused to face the fact that drug use had made me so unstable I couldn't hold a job. So I just smoked up.

This was a real low point. I had no income. There was no electricity or running water.

Standing out on the stoop one day, I had this sudden mental picture of myself. I was stuck in a revolving door. Going no place. If I didn't make some kind of good move, I was going to be out on the streets like a bum.

I also envisioned my beautiful daughter, some day in the future, coming around the neighborhood in search of me. I could hear her asking for me—and feeling ashamed at the responses. "No, I haven't seen that bum. But if you find him, tell him I want the money I loaned him." The thought that I would be a disgrace to her cut deep.

But why couldn't I stop what I was doing? Instead of being heartbroken I was getting more calloused. What was it going to take? My life was a blurred series of ugly snapshots.

I was smoking up right on the front stoop of the old tenement. My mind was flying. I just needed to go somewhere, anywhere. Without thinking, I waved down a passing cab. When the driver asked, "Where do you want to go?" I'd said, "Home."

"What's the address?"

I gave it to him, and he just looked at me.

"You *are* home."

"Take me *home,*" I shouted, getting violent.

"Get out of my cab," he roared.

Once on my way to buy drugs, I saw a commotion on the sidewalk. Pressing through the crowd, I saw a young guy writhing on the cement in a pool of blood. It was a drug deal gone bad, and the other guy had put a bullet in his head.

Ain't that just too bad, I shrugged. Why should I feel any remorse for him?

On another trip out to get drugs, I passed an alleyway, and smelled an awful decaying odor. Worse than usual. There, sticking out of a garbage can were pieces of a human body someone had cut up and just thrown away.

All I felt was—*nothing...*

Some time later, I was in a club doing cocaine and angel dust. A friend had just lost his mother.

"I just want to kill myself," he said over and over.

We were doing lines, and all I cared about was that he was messing up my good mood. "Why don't you shut up about killing your sorry self?" I said. "Everybody's mother dies. We're trying to have a good time here."

Eventually, I left to go up the block to get something.

When I came around the corner to the club again, there were cop cars with lights flashing, and a crowd. "Someone jumped off the roof," a guy told me. "What a mess."

The body under the white sheet was my friend.

That's when a voice inside my head said, *You were not raised like this. The life you've chosen is insane.*

Back in the dark apartment, I felt like I was coming apart. An emptiness opened inside me that was terrifying. I paced. I swore. I looked at the peeling paint and broken fixtures. Tears swelled, but I was too numb to cry. I felt like I was two steps away from insanity. The way I was living *was* insanity.

Taking some black shoe polish, I wrote on the crumbling plaster of a cold wall –*HELP.*

THE DREGS

Somehow, I talked my way into Grandma's new apartment. My cousin had returned to live with her, too. If Grandma had one thing, it was love. And that was about to be sorely tested.

One day, when I knew her church ladies were coming over for a prayer meeting, I worked her for some cash. These were the spiritual "mothers" of the church and I cleaned the place real good.

As Grandma handed me bills from her purse, she looked me straight in the eye. "Don't you use this money to buy that stuff you smoke."

"Okay, Nana," I promised, "I won't."

Down on the street, not twenty minutes later, I got some dust and smoked up. When I walked back in the door, I was high and felt myself climbing higher by the minute. My cousin saw my eyes. "Oh, no. The ladies are here. You better not let Nana see you."

Quietly, I snuck past the living room where the old women sat with open Bibles in their laps. Closing the door to one of the bedrooms, I flopped on the bed. I was soaring now. Sweating, I peeled off my clothes…

That was the last thing I remembered, until I woke up in bed with Grandma and all the old women standing around me praying. Apparently, I'd walked right into the middle of the prayer meeting without a stitch of clothes on and passed out on the floor. I can't imagine how these old women hauled me to my bed. But I could understand why Grandma looked like she was dying a thousand deaths.

Days and weeks blurred. I was smoking so much dust that I couldn't do reefer any more. So my use of dust picked up a lot. It didn't bother me that under its influence I became irrational.

Not long after, I tracked Grandma down at the apartment of one of her friends who lived just downstairs. She'd gone there to practice a song for church with three other elderly women. Only later would I learn that when the door opened, I staggered inside and crawled into the woman's bed. Raving, out of my mind, I kept calling out to these saintly old ladies to come hop in bed with me and I'd make them glad they did.

When Grandma told me later what I'd done, her beautiful old face was lined and drawn with deep, deep soul-sadness. I'd humiliated her in front of her friends. "I have no happiness in my own home," she said wearily. How could I go on hurting this dear lady, who had loved so much and lost so much?

When I wasn't feeling bad about hurting Grandma, I also had a good chuckle with my friends about the "old lady incidents." But still some bad and sobering stuff was going on all around me with people who were taking drugs.

Under the influence, one girl put her baby in a lit oven.

Rap music was just catching on, and the parties were getting wilder. More violent, too. Gang shootings were a threat at almost any party you went to, and I started avoiding those uptown Harlem scenes in favor of clubs downtown or in the Village, where you stood less chance of taking a bullet.

Basically, all I wanted to do was make enough money to party. And spend it on the thing that was having more and more influence over my life: Angel dust.

New Man

There was *one* good influence in my life. An unlikely source of positive inspiration. Sometime right before my drug use escalated, I had been sitting out on the stoop of the old tenement listening to records. Grandma was still living there. From across the street, I saw a well-dressed man coming toward me, smiling. He had beautiful, naturally wavy black hair, a nice suit. I was thinking, *why is this dude smiling at me when he doesn't even know who I...*

But as he reached the sidewalk in front of me, my jaw dropped.

This man was my dad.

Upstairs, seated at Grandma's table, he told us he'd become a Christian and gotten off drugs thanks to help from a ministry called Teen Challenge. It would be a long time before he could get his life stable, so he and Grandma agreed it would be best for my brothers, my sister, and me to continue living with her. Whatever this Teen Challenge was, though, I was glad it had given me my dad back.

From then on, though, Dad tried to see me often. He also kept trying to get me to become a Christian. I kept thinking, *you need that because you were a heroin addict for twenty years. I'm not in the kind of shape you were in.*

Sure, Dad was a new man. I could see that. But without realizing it, I was already falling into the kind of mental "pecking order" drug users have. Everybody who smokes pot thinks, *at least I don't do cocaine.* Coke users think, *at least I don't do heroin.* The beginning heroin users think, *at least I'm not a street-bum addict.*

Soon, Dad married again. He and his new wife lived in New Jersey. She was a wonderful Christian woman and a volunteer with the Teen Challenge program. With her, Dad eventually had a new daughter and a son. My sister moved to New Jersey with him, but I stayed in Harlem. Even as my life started to derail, just like Dad's life had, I marveled at the change in him. He was like a man who'd come back from the dead.

Seeing how he was trying to raise his new family made me feel proud of him. He had really changed, and I wanted to see him succeed.

Sometimes Dad came back to Harlem with a whole team of other Christians to give out clothes and Bible tracts. Occasionally, I'd go visit him in New Jersey and stay a few days. He certainly was no fool, and knew right away I was on drugs.

"Son," he said, shaking his head, "I know what you're doing. It's no good."

But Dad didn't press. I suppose his strategy was just to befriend me because he didn't want to lose me again. That was smart. If he'd pushed, he would have. As it was, I blew off all Dad's well-intentioned warnings.

Now, milking off Grandma, I sometimes thought back to all the times in the last couple of years my dad had tried to warn me about what I was doing to myself. Once in a while, I'd think, just for a few minutes, *if only I'd listened....*

Then I'd get high again. Why didn't I have enough sense to spare myself what lay just ahead?

Roller Coaster

What followed was a series of peaks and dips. Sometimes I'd manage to pull myself up a little. First, of course, I'd cut back on dope. Not quit. Just cut back. I'd get a job. I got my GED, and went for some college-level training. During these times, I'd feel like my life was happening again. I'd even land really good jobs at great places like the World Trade Center and Chemical Bank. After the "ups" came the "downs."

As soon as I felt in control of my life again, I'd slide back into heavy partying. More angel dust went in my lungs, and more cocaine went up my nose, than I can even remember. Time and time again I'd leave work, grab something to eat, hit a round of parties, and wake up the next day around noon, having blown off another morning at work.

It was amazing how much garbage I could come up with to excuse my absence to my boss. A sudden illness. A family emergency. A dentist's appointment ("I was sure I told you about that"). In the end, my erratic work record and undependable habits always got me fired. I was taking in a lot of drugs. I definitely could not see that each dip was taking me lower and lower again. The ride was getting rough again real fast.

With each passing day, a dull feeling was growing inside me. Not so much a feeling as a sense of emptiness. Outwardly, I was still partying. But inside—the times of sheer emptiness were scary.

As I sat in Grandma's house, stoned or depressed, I could see I was worrying her to death. Once, I overheard her praying in her room, crying out to God, "Please, don't let my grandson go to hell." That really jammed my conscience awake: *God forbid that she dies with me in this state. I'd carry that guilt for the rest of my life.*

I also discovered that my dad had told her, "Put him out of the house. As long as any of us keeps helping him, he'll never hit bottom and seek the help he needs." But she had told him, "He's a *son* to me. I can't do that."

Now I was the one on my knees. "God," I begged, "please help me to stop hurting my grandmother." But it was no use. In an hour or so I was thinking about getting my next high. I did come up with one solution. This would fix everything.

There was this big, restless dream in me. A hope that literally soared to great heights. I wanted to be in the Air Force. Even though it was competitive, I was sure I could get in. Where the desire came from, I don't know, but I wanted to be a chaplain. In any case, things were not working out in the business world.

The news came through in late summer 1980: The Air Force had tentatively accepted me. Grandma lost no time bragging to the neighbors. Everyone was thrilled. I was on my way up to a new life!

On the September morning I showed up at the enlistment office, I had my packed bags with me. A few last hurdles, and I'd be on a bus *out of here.* They'd told me I'd train in San Antonio, Texas. In every sense, I was ready to fly!

Then I stepped on the scales. I'd been warned the Air Force enforced strict weight limits, but I'd partied through the whole summer. The guy checking me out slid the weights across the scale's balance bar not once, but twice, then scribbled something on his pad.

"You're over the weight limit, son," the recruiting officer told me. I smiled. "Hey, just give me a couple hours. I can go out and jog off the water weight." But it was a no-go. "You were given the weight limits when you signed up," he said flatly. "The Air Force expects you to take it seriously. Apparently, you didn't. Sorry, but there are no exceptions."

They offered me another ship-out date a few months later. But I was devastated. All the way back to Harlem I cried like a baby. I'd thought I was escaping this place and my miserable life—but it had pulled me right back. In my mind's eye, I pictured myself as a guy who was reaching for a high goal—but I didn't have what it takes... and it slipped out of my grasp. It couldn't have been worse if they'd taken a rubber stamp and stamped my forehead with the word "Rejected." I was going home in humiliation and defeat.

Now the ground fell out from under me inside. The only things I'd ever had to hold onto all my life were *outside* me. Money, drugs, friends, the party-guy image. *Inside* there was nothing. Dreams blew away, and every day I plunged further into a pit of emptiness.

In a month, my whole personality changed. Disappointment turned to depression. All I knew to do to get out of my sorry self was to throw myself deep into drugs.

It was a quick slide down. *Numb* is the only word to use for where I lived in the coming weeks. Numb from cold. Numb from the inside. Numb as snapshots of reality blurred in together with my cocaine highs.

Pulling Out of the Death-Dive

There was only person on earth I believed I could turn to. I knew it would not matter to him what I was doing. His love was free, without condition or reserve.

When I showed up at Dad's door, he and his new wife welcomed me in with open arms.

"You know what God did for me, son," he said squarely. "He helped get me off drugs." Even though I'd wanted to be a chaplain, I still wasn't sure about this God stuff. I had no intention of "getting religion."

But as my dad talked, something did happen inside me.

I saw myself. I saw my dad talking to me the way a loving father *should* talk to his child. And I felt all the lost years when drug use had kept us from having this relationship.

And more than that, I saw my beautiful little Tia. Five years old now. I saw that I'd fallen into the same lifestyle and repeated the cycle—subjecting her to the same abandonment and neglect. I broke. No way was I going to put my little daughter through that kind of degrading humiliation.

Desperate as I was, willing as I was to change, I had serious doubts. Even with Dad—a living miracle—sitting right there in front of me, handing me tissues to wipe my eyes, I couldn't believe I could ever change. Harlem had been my family. My life. Harlem *had* me. And I didn't think I could ever escape.

"Just this once, son," my father said, reaching out his hand for mine, "don't try to go it alone. You've always had to make your way alone. You've had to be self-sufficient. Do it all on your own.

"If you can find it in yourself—I'm asking you, son—open up just this one time. Let someone get inside to help you. Reach out to something beyond yourself."

FROM DOUBT. . . TO DAWN

When I walked in the doors of the Teen Challenge center in Brooklyn it was a cold January morning. I had some hope, but also some serious doubts.

This was the same center my dad had gone to years before. These people, whoever they were, had helped to bring about a major change in a man who'd been a hopeless heroin addict for *years.*

On the other hand, I knew enough about drug addiction to know that you had to be really desperate and want help to *get* help. I'd known people who tried to get "cleaned up" enough to manipulate their boyfriend, girlfriend, or spouse back or to keep a job. Drug addicts are incredible liars and manipulators, and I was no exception.

What am I really here for? I asked myself secretly. I wasn't sure I knew.

I did know that for the first two weeks I was at Teen Challenge, I felt a stirring of something new inside. Mixed in with the doubt was a small bit of *happiness.* Maybe it came from the fact that for the first time in a long time, I wasn't lying or manipulating. It felt unbelievably good to be confronted with reality and to be *honest.* When did I let go of that value? And why?

It was important that I get out of the city, and an opportunity opened up for me to go to a Teen Challenge center called Camp Champion, in upstate New York. The director was Don Wilkerson, the brother of Teen Challenge's founder, David Wilkerson. I jumped at it.

At first, the doubts roared in at me big time.

First, Camp Champion was set in a natural and pristine environment. Beautiful. But it was definitely not the streets of Harlem, the only world I really knew. I was unsure, and that added to the anxiety.

Second, I was surprised when a load of guilt came down on me. I was getting a break. A lot of friends weren't getting this chance. Every morning as I woke to the quiet sound of a fresh breeze and birds singing, I could picture the friends who were no doubt smoking up in a hallway of a tenement somewhere. My own mom had died of heroin—she never got her break.

And along with those doubts was the big question: I'd been on drugs so long, *would I make it?* I still remember the day the change began inside me. The day when my doubts about making it began to clear, replaced by the first lights of a new dawn inside me. It was only a stray remark by a counselor in the midst of a longer talk—but it exploded inside me:

"People who are hooked on drugs or alcohol tend to see things only from a self-centered point of view. They tend to see all the bad things life handed them. Everything that was denied them. Sure, a lot of us had really, really bad things happen to us. But we also tend to overlook all the good things that God and other people did for us every day."

In my mind's eye, there was Grandma. Struggling, working hard to support us all against the toughest odds. I'd always thought about how lousy it was to lose my mother and have no father around. There was Grandma and my aunt, loving, sacrificing their whole lives for me and the other kids. And I'd stolen from Grandma, used her, lied to her. And there were Grandma's friends, who'd prayed for me for years.

Something was stinging my eyes as the counselor went on talking.

And there was a guy named James. I'd met him at the World Trade Center. He was as sold out to God as anyone I'd ever met. He'd befriended me. Told me about God's love. Taken me to church so I could turn my life around. And there was Martha, a co-worker I'd hit on at Chemical Bank. She resisted those efforts because she was a Christian, but had cared about me and prayed for me nonetheless.

It hit me. Through these people, and others who flooded my memory, God had been trying to love me and reach to me for years. I'd been too self-centered to see it.

Now, thanks to the godly people at Teen Challenge, I was being given the right perspective to look at my life.

That was the moment doubt began to go and a new light began to dawn. In that quiet moment, I bowed my head and prayed—surrendering my life, finally, to God.

HEALING. . . GROWING

The thing I learned very quickly about drug addicts was this: While we were on drugs, pretty much all our interior growth *stopped.* When you're that focused on yourself, and on getting the next hit, *and* on using other people and their money for your own ends, you don't have time for the healthy maturity that comes from getting involved in good relationships with other people. The kind where you learn to share life by learning to give as well as take.

This is where Teen Challenge did some very important things for me.

First, it gave me the chance to literally get out of my old setting. That alone cleared my head. But along with that, these good people challenged me to take a look at my life from the outside. *How did I relate to people? How did I use people? What did I really do that was of any use or value to other people?*

My main answer to these questions really stung. *Mostly I was focused on myself and my own good time. I hadn't cared about Grandma. Not even myself, really.*

What I felt was a good sting—like putting medicine on a nasty, infected sore. What made it bearable was that, along with the challenge, the Teen Challenge people assured us over and over that God is quick to show mercy and forgiveness when we're finally honest about our lives and ourselves.

As I stopped excusing my misuse of other people, I could almost feel my soul healing more every day. Becoming alive and human again.

There were so many other things I got from my time at Teen Challenge. Besides the spiritual guidance and drug counseling, there was something else about these people I couldn't quite put my finger on.

Once, on a weekend's pass home, I fell right back into drug use. When I returned, I thought they might give up on me. Maybe even kick me out of the program.

"Actually," the counselors told me, "*we* knew where you were in terms of kicking this stuff. But *you* needed to know where you were."

I could hardly believe the insight and wisdom—not to mention the grace they used in handling me. And still, there was something more.

I was nearing the one-year mark as Christmas 1981 rolled around. The director invited us all over one evening. There under their tree was a nicely wrapped gift box. I tore the paper off my package and inside was an expensive sweater. My mouth fell open.

That's when I recognized what it was about these people that was helping to change my life. It was *love.* Along with everything else I was receiving at Teen Challenge, I was loved.

To this day, more than twenty years later, I am thankful that God loved me enough to deliver me from drug addiction. His power—the healing power of love—reached out and gave another chance to a kid who began life without much of a chance.

I'm thankful, too, that He opened my eyes so that I could see His love coming to me through the men and women of Teen Challenge. To God, and to them, I am eternally grateful.

◆ ◆ ◆

Insight for Us All

Today, Floyd Miles is one of the most gracious, wise, and loving men you'll ever meet—and he's the founding Director of the Teen Challenge Center in New Haven, Connecticut. He is happily married to Mary, whom he met in Bible school. They have three children (Jeane, little Floyd IV, and Tyler) and remain close to Tia, who is married and living in South Carolina. Through him, God's light shines into the lives of men and women who feel—as he once did—that there might be no chance to turn their lives around.

If we consider Floyd's experience, there's a lot it can teach us all. First, Floyd's story says a lot about the trap that our silly human pride can create. At one point he describes the "pecking order" mentality many drug users have. He excused his cocaine use, telling himself, "At least I'm not a heroin addict."

The fact is, if you're using drugs, your mindset is altered. You've already moved the boundary line well away from the rational thinking zone.

Are you taking drugs and telling yourself, "I'm only doing pot, and not coke"? Do you rationalize it by saying, "Okay, so I may use drugs, but at least I'm still getting the kids off to school or holding down a good job"? Are you telling yourself, "Because I'm not as bad as someone who's using crack, I'm not so bad"?

It's time to face the fact that drug use always alters your sense of reality. If you're using drugs, the measuring stick you're using to gauge how "good" or "bad" you're doing is already out of whack.

The truth is, substance abuse will also make you push the line further. At some point, you will think you can handle more. As the drug you're using fails to give you the same high, you'll decide it's time to switch from what you're using now to something else that will give you a "better high." You'll tend to believe that because you're "handling" one drug "okay," you'll be able to handle another drug also without being affected.

There's a second really important message we get from Floyd's story:

If you or someone you know is involved in drugs, "reparenting" may be a very important key to recovery. As we saw, Floyd was given very little in the way of helpful parenting. For all practical purposes, although he had love, he raised *himself.*

Many psychologists and social workers will say that it's nearly impossible to re-parent someone once they get beyond the teenage years. Secular wisdom says that it's almost impossible to help someone to grow out of childish self-centeredness and immaturity once it's deeply patterned into their behavior.

But Floyd and many others who come to Teen Challenge find an all-important mix of unqualified acceptance and support *together* with challenge and training in discipline. Teen Challenge was able to do the job that the absent and busy adults in Floyd's early life did not do. In part that came through counseling, and in part it came through the "extended family" kind of relationships that begin at Teen Challenge and last for a lifetime.

Third, Floyd discovered that sometimes people come to drug treatment programs for the wrong reasons. Sometimes they come in order to manipulate or fix something in the world around them. Maybe they come in an attempt to win back a loved one, or to get a job back. Sometimes, it's just to satisfy a court mandate. It's true. Some people just want to clean up a little so they can say, "See, I'm really okay now."

Teen Challenge's huge success comes from going to the deep core with people. Its spiritual approach helps men and women see through their own manipulations. To become free of the tendency to manipulate and impress others is deeply empowering. And for those who are ready to let go of this unhealthy way to relate to others, it leads to long-term change.

One of the most moving aspects of Floyd's story is that he eventually recognized the seeds of love that had been sown by others in his life. Are you the one who has been loving, reaching out to someone on drugs? Does it seem like nothing is happening? While only God can open someone's heart, allowing those seeds to fall inside and take effect, *God is in the heart-opening, heart-changing business!*

At Teen Challenge, we can attest to that fact. Every day, as people are delivered of drug use and their lives change, we get to see the love and prayers of thousands rewarded.

Take heart. No matter how difficult it may look right now, *never give up.*

On the other hand—has someone been loving you, praying for you, reaching out to you to help you get off drugs? How long will you go before you let their seeds of love and kindness begin to open your heart to change? Just how long are you planning to wait before you give in, admit you need help, and then *get* help?

Maybe you or someone you know seems to have little chance of making it out of drug use or the poor lifestyle they're in. *It's time to hand your doubts to God.* Why not take a moment right now, and pray? Ask God to replace your doubts with hope and faith. Ask God for the courage to believe that with His help all things are possible. What we at Teen Challenge know is this: You will discover that God is the One who can always make a way when there seems to be no way. *Count on it!*

CHAPTER FOUR

"A REAL HARD CASE"

— Josh Fulton —

Floyd Miles, whose story we read in the previous chapter, started out life in a very rough place. He didn't seem to have much of a chance. Teen Challenge is successful in helping turn around people like Floyd because it offers hope and vision and a *new chance* at life.

But dealing with someone who's been given very little chance to make it in society is a different ballgame than dealing with someone who's a *real* hard case. Maybe you know the tough kind of person I mean—the one whose insides are made out of case-hardened steel.

Josh Fulton was that kind of guy. He came from a good home with well-educated parents who watched helplessly as their son turned into an angry rebel and a violent career criminal. With a police rap sheet as long as your arm, there was no reason to believe a guy like Josh could ever turn his life around, much less be transformed in spirit. What makes a guy like Josh turn into a stubborn and violent thug? More important, what penetrates that hard heart and opens it up to profound change?

Josh tells us in his own words.

MEET JOSH FULTON

We were traveling again. This time, we'd be seeing Paris—the Eiffel Tower, Notre Dame, and the great art museums. I was only five or six, and already my father's job with the U.S. diplomatic corps had placed us in New Delhi, India, before moving us along to Europe. My parents were excited that they were able to give me a chance to see the world at such a young age. No doubt, my father dreamed of me growing up to become a young sophisticate, maybe attend an Ivy League school and become a professional who, like him, had a positive influence on the world.

Maybe it was that Dad's career demanded so much travel, but they made the decision pretty quickly I was going to be their only child. As for me, of course I enjoyed the attention and the great life we were living! We would tour Europe, land briefly in the Midwest, then settle in a suburb just outside Washington, D.C., all before I turned ten. The neighborhood we landed in, in historic Mount Vernon, Virginia, was pretty upscale. For the most part, we were focused on all the Washington insider news Dad was privy to, and on plans for future travel to the world's wonderful places.

Dad had a great career path ahead of him, and if I just followed in his steps, I'd grow up to be a decent citizen and a successful professional, too. But that is not the path I would take.

CURVE BALL

There was a clear moment when life changed, when all our plans for a future full of sure success and an exciting lifestyle fell apart.

I was about twelve when I came home from school to the bad news. Dropping my books on the kitchen table, I went into the living room where Mom and Dad both looked white as ghosts. I knew Mom wasn't feeling well. But Dad was the one who looked nauseous at the moment.

"Son," Dad said, after motioning me to sit down. "It's not good news. Your mother has cancer."

I didn't know exactly what it meant that Mom had breast cancer. Or how serious her condition really was. I figured out how serious it was by how much things changed overnight.

Suddenly, my parents' focus changed entirely. There were weeks of doctors' visits. Then months of surgeries and treatments. And lots of serious and hushed conversations that excluded me. Even after the doctors told my dad they'd gotten all the cancer and Mom would be fine, nothing went back to being the way it was. Cancer was definitely the big curve ball that set our life on a different course than my parents had planned. It also helped to drive a really big wedge between my parents and me. Not that it was the only thing.

True, treating Mom's cancer took a lot of time and energy away from the demanding hellion my folks were trying to raise. Who could fault them, though? They were fighting for Mom's life. But not long after the cancer struck, puberty struck too. As a kid entering junior high, my head was scrambled with a lot of confusion. So many new pitches kept flying across my plate all at once. There was a new school, new kids, a new "dress code." How was I supposed to act? Mom's cancer returned suddenly, and she had to have a second breast removal surgery. Suddenly, the doctors' confidence that Mom would survive dwindled—and there was talk of the cancer spreading throughout her body. How was I supposed to feel about Mom? About the future?

My emotions rocked between anger and frustration—pretending nothing bothered me... and the desperate hope that my Mom would be okay. And in the roller-coaster ride of all these moods, Dad and I found ourselves locking horns in one battle after another. Not that I ever had a long fuse to begin with, but he could say or do something simple—like "Josh, why did your math grade drop?"—and it would set me off on a shouting fit.

That brings up school. I was doing terribly. Everybody noticed, of course, that I'd gone pretty quickly from being a kid with pretty good grades to a kid with lousy grades. My guess is Dad and my teachers explained it to themselves, in part, as a consequence of Mom's illness. And in part because I'd become really active in sports. The same strong-headedness that got me into fights with Dad carried over to the football field and my track meets—and I'm sure Dad was a little relieved to see my willfulness channeled in some healthy outlets. He didn't know, of course, about the unhealthy ones.

Rebel Without a Cause

The same bullheadedness that got me in trouble at home also got me a lot of friends. Being a rebel without a cause became my M.O. In the neighborhood and at school, I was the guy who'd try any crazy or dangerous stunt that came into his head.

My father had bought me a mini-bike. One day, riding it around with some of the neighborhood guys, I noticed that a guy down the street, an FBI investigator, had parked his Cadillac at the curb. I got an idea. Using some boards, I laid a "ramp" up one fender. Imagine the FBI guy's shock and anger when he came out to see what the hooting and cheering was about—only to find me playing Evel Knievel and jumping my mini-bike over his car!

One of my friends' dads was a firefighter. Someone—probably me—lit a fire behind a local school so we could see the fire company pull up with sirens and lights blaring and put it out. In one way, the things I did were just childish pranks. Crazy fun. But they were also out of the box. And in fact, the more crazy stuff I got away with, the more I began to push the edge. Even if I got caught.

More than once, I *did* get caught. Dad would try to send me downstairs to my room, threatening all kinds of restrictions. But by now—at just twelve years old—my rebel spirit was strong enough that I took charge of the scene.

"You can't tell me what to do!" I'd shout, getting in his face.

"Son," he'd counter, strongly, "get down to your room!"

"Make me!" I'd shout right back.

For all the tension and shouting, so much was left *un*said. Under it all, I was terrified about my mother. Inside my ribs was this gaping emptiness. The feelings were so huge, I didn't know how to say in words what was bothering me. I hated these feelings, hated being alone with them, so I kept busy all the time.

No doubt the uncertainty and fear were swallowing Dad alive, too, because he didn't seem to know how to talk about it either. This was 1970, and there wasn't a lot of counseling and help for the families of cancer victims.

And so the earthquake of Mom's cancer opened a big chasm of silence between us. Dad stood on one side, and I was on the other.

Poor Dad. I couldn't even tell him how bad I felt for him. How could he handle the overwhelming stress of Mom's cancer *and* a kid going wild, too? Also the stress of wondering when and how his one and only kid had slipped so totally out from under his authority?

So we'd fight. And Dad would just stare at me, with a mix of anger and mystified hurt on his face. And I'd glare back at him.

Bucking the System

Most definitely, I took advantage of my parent's preoccupation. I can't say what quirk inside of me knew enough to take advantage of the situation. But I did. Before junior high was over, I already had a lot to hide.

Around the neighborhood, I'd been hanging out with a bunch of guys who were renegades like me. Most of the guys were older—sixteen or seventeen. We called ourselves "the Buck Brothers" because every one of us was determined to buck the system. I was not quite thirteen when Jack, the older brother of one guy, came back from Vietnam. When I walked into their house one summer afternoon, I was greeted by a strange sight. Jack was holding a match under a tablespoon, heating something up.

"What the heck is that?" I asked. The guys rolled their eyes and laughed. I'd never even smoked a cigarette, or gotten drunk, like the rest of them.

"It's *dope,* you dope. Brown Mexican heroin. Wanna try a hit?"

Jumping a guy's Cadillac with a mini-bike only gets you so much status. These guys were fast moving out of my league. No way was I going to let the front edge move on without me.

"Sure," I said quickly.

Only a minute or two after the needle-stick, something really big happened inside me.

There was a rush in my head and tingling through all my veins. Best of all, the pit inside me was gone. All the terror and insecurity washed away in a flood of peace. By fall, when school started, I wanted to do dope all the time. Whenever someone had it available, I'd skip out of classes, go to their house, and shoot up.

Overnight, I'd become—for all practical purposes—a dope fiend. This was the *other* big reason my behavior toward my parents changed and why the gulf of silence grew between us. I had a big secret to keep. Within about a year of my first hit, when I was fourteen, I made the conscious decision that I'd do whatever it took to shoot up every day. In 1973, stuff was everywhere.

Of course, the adults in my life noticed the change. My grades tanked. I sat in the back of every class and heckled. No way was I going to obey or conform to anyone's rules. At least through junior high I'd been a little bit receptive. Now a steel wall went up between me and anything that remotely resembled authority. Amazingly, the adults around me also took my rotten attitude in stride. They labeled it "adolescence." They discussed "the fact that Josh is testing the limits of his masculinity searching for his identity." A few notes went home from school, saying, "Josh is distant" or "distracted."

My mom was experiencing a good period, as far as her illness. And so my folks were feeling up. They were focused on living again, and entertaining a lot. By now, they had their world, and I had mine. When they read the notes from school, they were concerned, but didn't know how to approach me anymore without triggering a shouting match. So they'd sit me down and ask, "Are you okay? Is anything going on?"

"Nope."

That answer stonewalled every attempt they made to find out what was wrong. I didn't *want* them getting into my world and learning what was up. I'd bucked my way out of their "system," and I wasn't going back. The odd thing was, I could still let myself feel a closeness with my mother if I wanted to. But the cancer could come back at any time—and I didn't *want* to feel close. Losing her would hurt too much. Along with shutting my parents out of my personal business, I also made the conscious decision to shut myself off emotionally.

If only someone had questioned more. Pushed me for honest answers. I, and my family—and a lot of innocent people—might have been spared.

Dropping Out

Only fourteen, and I felt full of myself.

If something was cutting edge and dangerous, I went for it. Using more and more dope made me cool. It also settled the worries and tensions I didn't want to talk about.

The thing is, while I thought the crowd of dopers I ran with were the "elite," we were kidding ourselves. See, there are no social expectations from other dope-shooters. The standard is not how "high" can you go—but how low can you go? Of course, I didn't view it this way then, but seeing who can get the most wasted is not exactly the highest standard.

At this point, my parents started to press me. I was a sophomore, and they asked me what I wanted to do with my life. What I wanted was to hang out and not have any responsibility. I didn't want to grow up. It felt too scary to assume responsibility.

With my friends I was all guts and a big mouth. But when I was alone I felt scared and confused. I didn't want to think about responsibility. What if I tried and failed? What if I didn't have what it took? Those were uncomfortable feelings. It was easier to get high and not face the discipline of growing up, working, delaying gratification.

A few friends, who were aware I was shooting up, did try to confront me. "What are you doing, man?" they'd ask. But then they got into dope, too. And so, in 1974, just before my fifteenth birthday, I made another conscious choice. I didn't want to have responsibilities. I didn't want to face the pressure that comes with living a responsible lifestyle. I sure as heck didn't want the pressure of anyone telling tell me what to do.

Looking at myself in the mirror one morning, I thought about my parents' question: *What are you going to do with your life?* And I decided: *From now on, I'm going to shoot up all the time.* Before my sophomore year was over, I dropped out of school. I'd go into downtown D.C. with friends, buy heroin, and shoot up.

Now my parents confronted me. Dad was upset and confused. Mom was crying.

"What are you doing, son?"

"I'm not doing anything."

"Josh, you're not going to school. You've got to go to..."

And I'd be calm for about the first five minutes. Then as the interrogation got more threatening, I'd just get nuts.

"Get off my back!" I'd shout, going off at them.

Intimidated, they'd let up. Maybe they were scared I'd do something even crazier. Or that I'd run away. In any case, it was way too late to try to rein me back with gentle persuasion and pleading.

I began staying away from home. Living downtown with friends in flophouse kinds of apartments in southeast D.C., the toughest section of town. Lots of things attracted me to the "bright lights and big city." Mainly, I'd developed connections and friends. Here I was close to my dope sources. And there were a lot of misguided girls who were attracted to me because I was the "bad boy" crazy type of guy.

Jack, the guy who'd first shot me up with heroin, had become a huge marijuana dealer. His brother was big into selling reefer. I was one of the boys, and I'd front fifty to a hundred pounds of reefer a week, and made a ton of money. But the angry energy I felt inside me was uncontrollable now. I wanted more. More money. More drugs. More danger.

Outside the Law

Life became one big party and one scheme after another. First it was trying to figure out where to get the best dope. Then, who we could steal from to get money to buy it.

I was sixteen when my buddies and I began robbing gas stations. In the 1970s, stations still had attendants, guys who'd come out to pump your gas carrying huge wads of tens, twenties, and fifties. While the attendant pumped, one guy would get the key to the men's room and disappear around the side of the station.

"Hey," he'd call out, "this key doesn't work. And I really gotta go."

The attendant would go around back to help him open the door, and three of us would run up and kick him square in the back. We'd shove him down beside the toilet and pound the heck out of him. We'd strip him of his cash and leave him so roughed up that we'd be long gone before he could stop shaking and call the cops.

We also began ripping off other dopers.

I'd go up to strangers in bars and ask, "What do you want?"

Maybe they'd say, "I need a supply of reefer."

"Okay, give me $350 and I'll get you a nice package. All you need."

Stupidly, they'd hand over the money and I'd scram.

Another scam I used was "the phone call." Once I met a kid from Oklahoma and got him talking until I found out he had an affection for cocaine. Then I made bogus claims about knowing this guy who had "*the* best stuff around." With the kid trailing me to a pay phone I placed a fake call. "Fast Eddie," I said to a time-and-temperature recording, "a guy here needs your best cocaine. I know you save it for your top clientele. But can you sell me some for this guy?"

When I stepped out of the booth, the dumb kid dished out all his cash.

"Good deal," I said. And just took off running.

The takes got bigger.

Once I had a guy meet me at the central bus station in D.C. He was carrying $12,000 and wanted to turn it into cocaine. "Driftwood" was with me—a six-foot-three monster who got his nickname from the fact that all he did was drift around.

"Here's the plan," I told the buyer. "You give me the money. I go into the bus station to a guy who's gonna pass me a key that opens a box. I put your money in the box, and I take out your cocaine. Then I come out and show you the stuff. If you like what you see, you keep it. If not, I go back in, put the cocaine back, and return your money."

"Okay," he shrugged. "Sounds good."

With $12,000 in hand, I went into the bus station… and right out the other side. Jogging up the street, I went to a friend's house where I placed some calls. *Thanks, sucker,* I thought, as I ordered a bunch of cocaine and heroin for my own little party.

Meantime, Driftwood sat in the guy's car with him as a half hour ticked by.

"You think he's coming back?" the guy said, turning to Driftwood.

"Nope," he said. And with one punch, he knocked the guy out cold. Big hauls like this one left us flush for a nice little while. We played the big men, and got all our friends high. Then the money ran out and we'd have to find someone else to do.

The takes also got more violent. We'd see guys out on the street dealing. It was common for these guys to have one or two hundred packages of heroin on them. We'd pull up like we were going to make a buy. Then I'd jump out and shove a gun in the guy's face. "Drop the packages," I'd shout. "Drop the money. *And* drop your clothes." When the guy was naked, I'd order him, "Now run down the street."

While the guy scrambled to find something to cover himself, we'd be long gone.

We also began to use girls we met. We'd have a girl meet a guy in a bar—a big wheeler-dealer type. A little flirting, and he'd take her home. When she saw what the guy had laying around—cash, dope—she'd have to make a "personal" call.

If the take was going to be good, I show up in a car with two other guys. By now the guy would be in no position to defend himself. Commando-style, we'd kick in the door and charge the guy with baseball bats and shotguns.

Frankly, we thought knocking over dope dealers and drug buyers was a beautiful plan. What were they going to do—call the police and report us for stealing their drugs and drug money? By seventeen, I knew I was the smartest bad guy around. And that was my downfall.

IT ALL COMES DOWN

Drugs and ego are a bad combination. I was riding high on both and thought I'd never fall. I was in this frame of mind when someone told me about a pharmacy down in Richmond, an hour and a half south of D.C. The info was that this place kept a lot of cash on hand, plus a large quantity of a pharmaceutical drug that was the equivalent of cocaine.

Pulling up to the pharmacy after dark one evening, I checked everything. The gun in my pocket was loaded. The lot was fairly empty—not too many witnesses. The roads were quiet too, so getaway would be easy.

When I flashed the gun in the pharmacist's face, the guy went pale. With shaking hands, he fumbled around with the drugs. This store was supposed to be loaded and I wanted the whole shot. I didn't want the cash; the drugs would be worth more on the street.

Back outside, I jumped in my car and shoved into gear. From out of nowhere, police cars surrounded me. Officers swarmed me, dragging me out, shoving me over the hood, handcuffing me. It was all over in seconds. Later, I'd learn that there was an alarm button under a mat the pharmacist stood on. I'd thought I was smart for making him keep his hands in sight while he pretended to fumble to give the cops more time to get here.

The next morning, in a Richmond jail, I faced my shaken dad and his lawyer. After some legal talk, Dad looked at me, with so much pain and sadness in his eyes. "I did the best I knew how with you. I lost you. You need to find a way to get yourself together, son."

I looked deep into his eyes. "Dad, I'll never do wrong again. Just help me."

What was wrong with me? While the words were on my lips, I knew I was lying and manipulating him.

The whole time I was in jail, awaiting trial, Mom never came to see me. Her cancer was back with a vengeance and seeing me behind bars would be too taxing. I was given a two-year sentence and sent to the Virginia State Pen. This was a truly nasty place, known as "the Walls." Up front they told me I could get off with less time—eleven months—for good behavior. If only I'd known the meaning of the term.

HARD HEAD

Being seventeen and stuck inside steel bars would be a wake-up call for most guys. But my head was pretty hard.

Things went from bad to worse when a guy tried to take my radio. I cut him with a knife. Now I was charged with attempted murder. And that caught me more prison time.

In the Virginia system, they added new time on top of old time. If you picked up a second sentence on top of your first one, you didn't have a chance to reduce that sentence with good behavior. You served it day for day and *then* you went back to counting down time on the first sentence. So more time was heaped on.

Here was my problem. Prison is a whole different world, with its own set of rules. Oddly enough, I'd never listened to healthy authorities on the outside. But it began to dawn on me that I was going to be in here a while and I needed to survive. So I began listening to the "sages" of the prison system—the guys who were in for twenty-, thirty-, or fifty-year sentences. They were the convicts, and they pretty much ran the prison. From these older guys, I started learning the principles of life behind bars.

For one thing, in the pen you've got to have the heart to take anything someone does to you to the next level—show him you'll do whatever it takes to defend what's yours. If you do to me, I do *much worse* to you. This is what you do to survive. This led me to more stabbings and assaults.

Another thing was, you had to stay "in the loop" if you wanted anything. You made "friends" based on what guys could do for you. The best thing someone could do for you was to help you get out of your head. Being caged makes you crazy. Everyone wants dope. If you want to stay in the loop, you have to have something to trade. So you get someone to sneak dope in to you. Hidden in the false bottom of a sneaker. Or a body cavity. Whatever. Some of the guards, who were looking for extra cash, could be bribed to bring stuff in to us, too.

Maybe the most important survival principle was that you *never* went over to the system's side. No matter how much the guards pushed you for inside information, you stayed on your side of the bars. The guards recognized my flash-fire temper and made it a game to taunt me, knowing they had the power to bust my head any time they wanted to. I knew it, too, and hated their guts.

So here I sat, stuck in a situation that, for a guy like me, was made in hell. I was supposed to working on "good time," to show I was being rehabilitated. But the prison environment pushes you to do things its way or else suffer in some pretty bad ways.

All in all, the system was stacked against a hardhead like me. I got slammed over and over again with new charges on top of old ones. Reefer sales. Beating up inmates. By 1978, I'd been in prison for two years. I hadn't seen my mom since coming here, and it didn't look like I'd be getting out soon.

One afternoon, I was keeping to myself, killing time reading a novel. I looked up and noticed a guard staring at me. I couldn't stand the guy to begin with, but today his smirk was really irritating.

I glared back. "What are *you* looking at?"

He chuckled. "Guess what, Fulton. Your mama got real sick today. And ya know what—she's *dead.*"

Anger, like a flash fire, was all over me—and I was all over him. Knocking him down. Strangling him. I didn't feel the other guards beating me with riot sticks until they pulled me off the guy.

They didn't even let me out to go to the funeral. I was—of course—facing another serious charge at the time. And even though my father said he would hire police to escort me, the prison officials thought I was a flight risk.

On the day my mother was buried, I sat in a cell. For all practical purposes, I might as well have been buried, too.

Inwardly, I was smothering in rage. Consumed in bitterness. No way did I associate the mess I was in with anything I'd done wrong. It was everyone else's fault.

The thought that I'd never see my own mother again—and that no one cared if I was even allowed to see her face one last time—nearly consumed me with bitterness. Bitterness against "the system." Against God.

My Own Worst Enemy

If it was possible, my heart got even harder.

My existence revolved around doping and scheming. There were charges on charges.

Before it was all over, I'd build an eleven-month sentence into *thirteen-and-a-half years* behind bars.

All the while my bitter hostility grew.

Sometimes I'd stay high for days. Then my supply would get shut down, and I'd be strung out. Sick. Shivering. Guards taunting me. No hope of getting to a methadone clinic.

I'd grit my teeth and commit myself even more to life as a dope-fiend. For all I cared, they could keep me locked up for life.

Now I lived by another principle of the pen: *Don't get attached to anything or anyone on the outside.* If you had outside contacts, say, with women, you just used them. You didn't get hooked on them or it would make you nuts.

I didn't even let myself get hooked. During one three-year period, I never made a single phone call or contacted anyone on the outside. As completely as possible, I cut myself off from needing anyone.

Some guys wanted to get out and work in the road camps. They'd tried me on that once and it didn't work. Me and another guy would end up controlling the camp and selling hash.

Now I didn't *want* to go out. I didn't *want* to see nice people driving by, doing their nice lives. I operated better in prison, among people who thought like I thought.

My only reality now was to be a predator. To use any situation and make it profitable for me.

A number of years after Mom died, my father came to see me. Our contact had been very infrequent. I have no doubt his pain was unbearable, seeing what his only son had become.

"Son, I'm going back overseas again." That was an indirect way of saying he had to move on with his life. I couldn't blame him, but I made out like I couldn't care less.

He'd also brought a "special friend" to meet me. A very lovely woman.

I have no idea what possessed me to hate this obviously fine lady on sight. Nothing about me was rational. All the circulating rage in me grew, until I wound up shouting at her, "If I ever see you again, I'll cut your head off."

As she fled screaming, I knew I'd signed my final warrant in Dad's eyes. How could he even come close to a son who seemed to enjoy working to drive everyone away?

Sure enough, weeks later, Dad's letter came. "Seeing you has become too painful. You've caused me so much deep hurt. I want to be there for you. But you don't even want that. I'm sorry..."

I was furious, not sorry. Who was he to disown *me*? I disowned *him*. But even in my cold hatred, I knew I would have done the same thing. It's all anyone could have done.

To my own father, I was dead.

Out, But Not Free

At midnight on January 13, 1993, I was released from prison. I'd been in Lorton, just outside Washington, D.C. Finally, after spending nearly half my life in prison, I'd paid my dues. I'd only wised up enough to get sick of prison and do some "good time" so I could get out.

As I walked out into the freezing January dark, I carried in the core of my being every ounce of bitterness and predatory hatred I'd gathered over every single rotten day for more than thirteen years.

Waiting for me in a car was a friend from prison. As I slid into the front seat, Rick threw thirty-three hundred-dollar bills in my lap. "What do you wanna do, boy?"

Good old Rick. Prison hadn't changed him any more than it changed me.

"I want to go up to Nineth and O," I answered, "and get me a bag of heroin and get messed up."

Within days of my release, I got hold of a car and a gun. I was "rippin' and runnin'" again.

Not one minute of my prison time had done any good in any way to change me.

One night, I'd copped a pack of dope out on the streets and was walking back to my buddy's car with it hidden in the palm of my hand. Some girl on a porch called down to me, asking to bum a cigarette. I waved at her and told her I didn't have one. Two cops, just down the block, happened to catch a glimpse—something concealed in my hand.

"All right, man!" they yelled, running up the sidewalk at me. "Give up the dope."

No way. I shoved the little bag in my mouth and swallowed it.

For that, they handcuffed me to a rail and beat me for the next thirty minutes.

With no evidence, of course, they let me go when the fun was over.

Around the corner, my partner was watching and laughing the whole time. I swore at him as he drove me to a store to buy shampoo. I gagged down most of the bottle, to make the dope work out. We finished the evening hustling for more dope to get cash—then picked up two ladies off the street and drove to New York Ave., where we got a hotel room for the night.

When I woke up the next morning, there was nothing remarkable about it at all. I was hung over. That wasn't new. There on the dresser was my pistol. A pile of cash. Bags of dope. Beside me, still asleep, was the prostitute I'd picked up.

Quietly, I went into the bathroom and used the john. Then I went to the sink to splash cold water on my face.

When I looked up, though, something happened. The face looking back at me was the face of someone I didn't know. Someone I suddenly didn't like.

From deep inside came the truth, as I saw what I was. And then the words, "I hate you."

As if someone had kicked me in the stomach, those words, coming from my own lips, woke something in me. I went back and sat on the edge of the bed. What good was all this stuff? What good was my whole life? I hated the sick predator I saw in the mirror. But how could I get away from him when I *was* him?

Feeling edgy, I threw on clothes. Then I woke up my buddy, still asleep in the other bed.

"Here's my pistol," I said. "Here's all the money. I'm keeping two dollars for the metro. I'm leaving."

"What are you doing, man?" he said groggily.

But I was out of there.

From out of nowhere, one thought pulsed through my splitting head. *Go see Ricky.* Rick was a guy who'd helped me "run" the road camp. He'd gotten out, got married, and opened a carpet store.

But I didn't *want* to see Ricky. The last time I'd heard from him, he'd gotten "saved" and talked to me about "Jesus." I didn't need *that.*

Okay, I thought, flipping back to predator thinking, *at least I can get a place to stay out of him.* Something was going on and I needed to get my head together.

Ricky was living with his wife and small son. Rough looking as I was when I banged on their door, they took me in. Immediately, I knew something in Ricky had changed radically.

In prison, you don't care about anyone. And if you're stupid enough to care, you sure don't show it.

Ricky's concern for me was genuine. They let me stay in their guest room, and Ricky slept out on the sofa. I knew it was because he was concerned I'd slip out in the middle of the night. Even if I got up at midnight for a cigarette, he'd stand outside with me.

"I'm *not* letting you go, man," he'd say. "Not until you get your head straight and get your life right."

The problem was, I was beginning to *feel* inside. And I'd think, *Yeah, like that's gonna happen.* What I felt was totally hopeless.

The Challenge

Ricky's plan for getting my head straight and my life "right" was to get me into a program called Teen Challenge.

Working it out with my parole officer, I traveled from D.C. to a Teen Challenge center outside Boston, in Brockton, Massachusetts. During the first evening of meetings, I sat in the back and watched as other guys talked openly about their feelings. As tears flowed, and guys hugged each other, I thought, *they wouldn't last five minutes in prison.* This looked weak and sick.

"How can we pray for you?" someone asked at one point.

"Um…" I stumbled, "…pray for me to get some wisdom." Everyone nodded earnestly. I knew they thought I meant wisdom about "getting my life right" and "getting right with Jesus." I meant wisdom about whether I should stay or get out of this place.

Truthfully, I hated every single minute of my first two months at Teen Challenge. The bitter rebel in me despised living by a schedule. And all this emotion and "honesty"—who needed that?

But I couldn't stop listening to what these people had to say. The men leading the Bible studies and group sessions were genuine. I knew a scam when I saw it, and there was no religious scam going on here. And I could tell good things were happening to other guys all around me—to men who'd been business executives, or gutter bums, and everything in between.

So I sat back and watched. Mentally, I had one foot in and one foot out of Teen Challenge. Something deep in me said, *if anything gets hairy or weird, or if someone gets too close, I'm outta here.*

One thing I watched—*closely*—was the guys leading this program. One was a guy named Floyd Miles, a former addict from Harlem. Another was Jimmy Vitale, who'd been another druggie burnout. These guys claimed that God had helped them stay clean for years. After coming from prison, where everything you said, and the mask you put on, all of it was a lie, I couldn't get where these guys were coming from. They were upfront, simple, honest, no lying.

With that old predator's eye for vulnerability, I watched to see if their lives matched what they said.

I also dug into the Bible. It had a lot to say about integrity. Being up front about what you are. Not hiding, running, scamming, doing other people. The people I'd hung with all my life told the truth *maybe* two percent of the time. I prided myself on telling the truth maybe three percent of the time.

To be truthful, the Bible was hard to get into. All those old names. Little numbers all over the pages. It was hard to think about the super-holy God this book talked about. But an odd thing happened. It seemed like God was saying something to me—that I shouldn't worry about understanding the Bible right now, and that I should go ahead and watch these Teen Challenge people very carefully. I'd learned in prison to watch people, to see how far you could trust them, to see what they were about.

In a sense, God seemed a lot like me. Like God was saying it was important to believe that people's *words* should match what they *do*.

Confronted with these thoughts, something began to happen inside me. With each passing day, I felt more uncomfortable. Not exactly with Teen Challenge but with *me*.

Just like that morning at the hotel back in D.C., I couldn't look at myself in the mirror without shouting inside, *I hate you, I HATE YOU!*

Now I was sure I was cracking up. Maybe it was this place. These people. They were making me think like a religious whacko. Maybe I needed to cut and run.

One morning, still unsure what I was going to do, I was shaving in front of a mirror when whatever it was that was speaking inside me seemed to reach out and grab me by the tee shirt.

So you want to run. What—? Just like you've always run? You've been ripping people off all your life, and running. That's pukey enough. But the thing is, you could have had a decent, honorable life with people who loved you. But you couldn't hack that. You ran from it. And you know what? The person you ripped off worst of all is yourself.

My hand was white-knuckling the razor, and I wanted to smash something. There was no one to hit, and that made me more frustrated.

I knew now why I hated myself. It was because I could trust myself only to be a liar, a thief, a thug. I could count on myself only to take advantage of every person who came near me in some way. I was no better than that—and I'd been given every opportunity to *be* better than that.

In the coming days, if I could have taken off my old life, my self, like a stinking, rotted shirt, I would have. My past was just a string of lies and broken promises. I wanted to run—but where do you run to get away from your *self?*

The man I wished I was, the man I wanted to be—I just couldn't believe *that man* could ever be me. Teen Challenge guys kept talking about becoming a "new man in Christ." But how could I dare to believe someone who was nothing but a manipulator and liar could ever speak one word of the truth?

For the next week, I was so lost in my own head, confused and hopeless—I didn't even know if I was lying to myself, just *saying* I wanted to change, right at that moment. All I knew was that I had to keep this crazy, confused thinking to myself.

After days of this mental torture, I knew what I had to do. It was all I knew *how* to do. And I didn't want anyone getting to me, like I was some weak chump, and talking me out of it.

PRISON BREAK

One morning in chapel, I knew it had to be today. I wasn't going to let this walled-in feeling, or this center, confine me one more day. I'd kept my decision a secret because I didn't want these guys slobbering all over in tears and praying for me.

Chapel ended, and the place emptied. Back in the room, my bag was packed. But for some reason I stuck to my seat. In a few minutes, two guys—Chris and Nicky—came back to find me. Each one laid a hand on my shoulder—and I hated that. And at the same time the thought came, *What's wrong with you, man? Why do you hate it so much when anyone tries to get close?*

"Come on, Josh," Chris said. "What are you waiting for? It's past time. You need to do business with God."

They began to pray for me. I hated this. It was exactly what I didn't want, because privately I was fighting back tears, willing them just to shut up and go away. And at the same moment, I sent out these heartfelt words. *Please… I'm asking you… change me. You know I can't do this big, open, public thing. Maybe it's not a show for anyone else—but it could turn into one for me. I can't be fake one more second of my life. So I'm begging you. Make some real change in me. If you can do that… change just one little thing… then I can believe you're real.*

When the guys finished praying, I had the feeling they were a little disappointed. I hadn't given them one sign anything was different. But it was.

Something inside me opened just a crack. I was ready to make a break from the prison I'd been in all my life—that hard, hard place

I called a heart.

At first, I didn't think anything had changed either. But for some reason I didn't leave.

Up until now, I had been watching the guys who led the program—Floyd, Jimmy, and some others—noticing they seemed pretty honest, but I'd been wondering what kind of scam they were running. Like maybe they just wanted to show us all how religiously superior they were to us degenerates. But now I found myself watching them for a different reason. I wanted to know where they got their obvious integrity from. And their love. These guys genuinely cared about us. What was that all about?

Then one morning, it dawned on me. Something inside me had changed. It was my perspective. In jail, I'd been a disciple of the prison convicts, and fashioned myself after them and their attitudes. But now I wanted to fashion myself like these Christian men. Something deep in my will had changed. It dawned on me that my prayer had been answered.

Alone in my dorm room one day, I realized something else. The day I'd been let out of the D.C. prison, I'd still been a total prisoner. The cage that held me was my old attitudes and ways of thinking.

Here at Teen Challenge, for the first time in my life, I'd been set free from the person I'd been.

Still, I kept the change inside me to myself. All around me, guys were claiming they were being instantly changed. Maybe so. I sure wasn't in a place to judge anyone. But I'd seen too many guys in prison scamming parole officers and guards, making a big show that they'd "changed" just to manipulate their way back to the streets.

Day by day, I kept changing, though. I felt hungry to learn from the Christian men around me. And if some guy in the program had a beef with a leader, I pretty much just wanted him to shut up. That was when I discovered that, besides wanting to be a man who could be trusted, I also didn't want to take people down anymore. All my life, I'd looked for weakness, and nailed it. Now I wanted to protect people, encourage them, and bring them up.

Sure, men were men. And leaders made some mistakes. But these guys could be doing *anything* with their lives—in business, or education. But they were spending their lives helping a bunch of hardhead addicts like me. Usually, they had to "pray in" funds just to survive. What could possibly be in this for them?

I listened to every word they said, and watched every action. I knew they meant it when they said stuff like, "Put other people before yourself. Because if you put them before you, they can't step on your toes."

At some point, I stood up in front of other people and told everyone I wanted to give my life to Jesus Christ, too. There were tears, and a lot of "praise Gods." But for me it was pretty unemotional.

Under it all, I felt some piece of me was held in reserve.

Even though I sensed some pretty big changes in myself, I wondered. Let's say I *did* want to live my life as a Christian now. Let's say I wanted God in my life.

How did I know for sure, after everything I'd done, that God really wanted me? So far I just had other people's word on it. I wondered what God really thought.

A Son Comes Home

As the weeks went on, I gained a little confidence about my new faith. I actually heard kind words coming out of me. Felt genuinely concerned for other people. Man, was *this* new! I was also inspired by the people all around the Northeast region who were on Teen Challenge's mailing list and who prayed regularly for all us guys. Some of us by name. Even though they'd never set eyes on us. I started to believe I could be successful.

Six months into the program, I was working with a crew of guys constructing a new building for the Teen Challenge center. As we were working, Jimmy Vitale sought me out. "While I was praying this morning, I believe God told me something. I believe there's going to be an office in this building for *you*."

I opened my mouth to say, "You're nuts." But something stopped me. Instead I mumbled, "Man, I don't know. I'm not even finished with the program."

What stopped me was a new conviction I had. Whether I was going to work with Teen Challenge, I couldn't say. But for the first time, I sensed there *was* a good plan for my life.

Still, that secret doubt about God's love for me lingered. I kept hearing I was completely forgiven, but all the images of all the people I'd hurt kept replaying. Becoming a Christian really *was* like becoming a new man—like someone coming back from the dead. Because all the guilt nerve endings were coming back to life.

Sometimes nothing but pain and anguish would roar through me for everything I'd done to people. I'd made the final years of my Mom's life a living hell, and hadn't even been at her side so she could have seen her only son's face one last time before she died. The day this truth landed on me, I broke and sobbed convulsively.

Most especially, I remembered Dad's face the last time I saw him. That last visit we'd had before he'd had to cut himself off to protect his wife—not to mention his own heart—from any more of my scams and brutal treatment. I'd sent some letters to him through a family member. But I'd heard nothing back. It killed me that I'd been a renegade, and I'd killed my own father's love for me.

And so it was that when Christmas 1993 came, I stayed in Brockton as the snow fell from gray skies and other guys went home for the holiday to see family. Two days before Christmas, the place pretty much emptied out.

After dinner, as evening fell, the dorm felt really cold. I was alone. Feeling more alone than I'd ever felt in my life.

For the first time, I also needed things and didn't have any way to get them. Now that I wasn't ripping people off any more, where was I going to get money for the clothes and other things I needed? I'd been thinking a new shirt would be nice. Maybe a sweater.

But with no family at all, and also no money, there weren't going to be any presents under my Christmas tree. There wasn't even going to be a tree.

I know I deserve this, I thought, *selfish jerk that I've been all my life.* Okay, so I seemed to be changing. But when you've spent your life taking and victimizing, who's left to treat you good when you really need it?

It was still snowing on Christmas Eve day, when someone knocked on my door.

"Hey, this package came for you." In his hands was a box.

The only person who could possibly have sent me a package was Ricky. But he and his wife lived in D.C.—not in Long Island, which is where the postmark on the box was from.

Alone on my bed, I opened the package. There was no card, no note. Just two oblong boxes in Christmas wrapping. *Maybe this is from one of those Christians out there who pray for us guys, but why?*

As the paper came off the first gift, and the box came open, my jaw dropped.

Inside was a shirt. A really nice silk shirt. Exactly what I would have picked out. And in my neck size and sleeve length exactly. *How on earth?* I thought, feeling mystified.

And in the next gift box was... *a sweater.* Exactly the color, exactly the style I liked.

Then it was all a blur of colors, as my eyes swam and overflowed. Grateful as I was to the anonymous giver who'd sent me these unbelievably perfect gifts, they'd done something for me that was far, far greater than they'd ever know.

In my hand I held what was to me a proof-positive message. It said, *Listen, I know every thought you think—everything you want and need. Even the most secret desires and feelings inside you. I know you.*

That was the day I knew. God had taken me, renegade that I was, into his own family. I felt like the prodigal son in the parable—the guy who'd blown everything given to him in his youth, until he deserved nothing but the pigsty he was living in. Like that other young fool, *this* prodigal had required some very hard knocks on the head in order to wake up to the truth.

All my life I'd run. But when there was no place left to run, I'd turned and found that wide-open arms were waiting for me. The arms of my new father who is God.

◆ ◆ ◆

Insight for Us All

Josh Fulton is one of those people whom you look at, and hear their story, and say, "You can't be the same guy you were just talking about. That's impossible." Today, Josh is the Director of the Teen Challenge Men's Center in Dorchester, Massachusetts. He has been married for four years to Cynthia, and is the proud father of Rebekka Joi.

You'll also be interested to know that God is really in the reconciling business. Josh and his dad are making headway in reconciling after all those lost years.

Josh's experience shows us pretty clearly why the prison system fails at rehabilitating people. He lived in a system where he had to act one way to survive, obeying the rules of prison life. And at the same time, people have to go through rehab groups and counseling and show they're getting "well" enough to get along on the outside again. Who can navigate a situation *that* full of unhealthy contradictions?

Apart from that general observation, there are some important lessons we can all learn from Josh's hard experience.

No doubt you picked up on the fact that Josh was as headstrong as they come. He pushed for independence and the right to live life by his own rules. He ignored every piece of advice and every warning. As a result, he got a life that was all of his own making—and a total mess.

First, here's a thought for each of us to consider: If someone is trying to warn you that what you're doing is going to get you in trouble—*listen up!* And if you're the one doing the warning—*stick with it!* Don't ever give up.

As one great writer has put it, there's nothing more terrible than a human will that's never been challenged. And nothing is more tragic than a life that's being wrecked by its own stubborn foolishness.

Second, we can see how Josh's parents let their son's bullheadedness open a rift between them and him. As so many parents do, they seemed to feel overwhelmed and unable to do anything to keep from growing apart from their child.

On the one hand (and who can blame them, given the invasion of cancer?), they became absorbed in their own world. Many of us get caught up in our own lives, even our own inner pain. But when we do so, we too often forget to maintain healthy relationships with our children.

On the other hand, many parents believe that teenagers need to separate from their parents, in the sense that they need to establish a healthy identity of their own. While there's some truth in this, we all need to grow up with the sense that we're not completely on our own, that we have interest and support, and also boundaries and accountability.

There were other people in Josh's life who might have intervened—teachers and principals, perhaps. Some of them obviously noticed serious changes. But beyond sending a note or two home, no one in authority stepped in—until he was way out of control.

The fact is, anyone with love and concern can have a healthy influence on someone who is losing his or her way and headed for disaster.

If you're the parent of someone who is on drugs, it's not too late—no matter what age your child is now—to reestablish the healthy parent-child relationship every one of us needs. If you are a school authority, or occupying some other leadership role in a young person's life, your interest *can* make all the difference. If you have the concern, the next question is, will you have the guts to reach out and try?

Third, it was interesting to see how Josh was using drugs to cover up the pain of his own emptiness—even when he wasn't consciously aware he was feeling emotional pain. This tells us you don't have be a "weak" person to experience a deep emptiness of soul. Apart from God, there is an emptiness inside each of us.

For that reason, we're all susceptible to trying something, *anything*, to fill that emptiness in some way. For some of us, it may be with money or success—for others, it may be with dependent relationships, or possession, and for others, with alcohol or drugs.

When we use drugs to fill the emptiness, we set ourselves up to be deceived. Because drugs alter brain chemistry, giving us the false peace of chemical euphoria, we *think* they've solved our problem. But it can't last. And on top of our first sense of emptiness, we've added another one—that bigger emptiness that substance dependency always gives.

As we saw in Josh's story, God is using Teen Challenge to break through even to the very hard cases. And inside those hard cases, He's working to close old wounds. At Teen Challenge, He works through a kind of prayer and counseling that brings men and women into God's presence so they can shoulder the responsibility at last for problems and conflicts they've run from for years.

Do you know someone who has run as far as they can go? Is it you? *What are you willing to do about it?*

CHAPTER FIVE

"WHO CARES?"

— Tom Parker —

As you read in the previous chapter, Josh Fulton often chose the hard way. Rebellion, a central part of the human spirit, goes back as far as the Garden of Eden. Josh's rebellion against his family, friends, and the strict rules of prison all contributed to a very hard life for him. He managed to build an eleven-month prison sentence into thirteen-and-a-half years!

Perhaps you know someone who rebels at all the things in his or her life. Is rebellion in control of *your* life?

Tom Parker, whose story is told in this chapter, was just an ordinary middle-class kid. Rebellion was not controlling him, but when catastrophe struck his family, he had no anchor to hold his life securely in place.

What can happen to a young boy whose world cracks apart? Does he have the ability, maturity, and resources to cope with this devastation, or will hopelessness lead him elsewhere?

MEET TOM PARKER

I can still recall the day when I was thirteen and life fell apart.

Ours was a lower middle-class neighborhood at the edge of Boston. Mostly Irish-Catholic and Italian-Catholic. My dad was a house painter. At least the modest wages he made didn't have to be split up among a bunch of kids, because I was an only child.

The day my life changed forever, I was sitting in class in Catholic school, trying to follow along with the nun who was teaching us English grammar. A knock at the classroom door interrupted, and when the instructor opened it, another, older nun was standing out in the hallway, looking very serious. Something was whispered, and then they were motioning to me.

What did I do now? I thought. I wasn't a bad kid, though I did get an occasional scolding.

"Come with me, Tom," the older nun said. And I began following her down the corridor.

"What's going on?" I asked nervously.

She hesitated, then stopped and faced me. Her eyes were compassionate. "I'm sorry, Tom. Your mother has sent a neighbor here to bring you home. She's down in the office. Your father passed away today, at work."

The jolt of despair I felt was awful. Pain shot through my chest.

I loved my dad. Even though he'd come home exhausted every night, and we never did a lot together, at least he believed in me. He had dreams for me. "You're gonna go far, Tom," he'd say. "I didn't get to go to college. But you're gonna. I want you to have the chance for college I never had."

I stood there, numb with grief. A million thoughts rolled through my head. Where was Dad now? What about Mom—how would she handle this?

And what about *me*?

At home, I found Mom in bitter despair. The gulf I felt inside me, then and at Dad's funeral, was huge. Empty.

With that one single turn of events, my life was up-ended. And I was soon to find that I was on my own.

Making My Own Way

Right after Dad's funeral, Mom began drinking. She was a hard worker, but when she came in the door after work, the bottle became her escape. Pretty much, our life stopped. We'd gone to the Catholic church up till now, but that ended. And so, inside, I had nothing to turn to.

I'd always been close to Dad, not so much with Mom. Now, as she buried herself in her job and the bottle, our relationship more or less died. There was no extended family at all, so there was no one to challenge Mom about what she was doing. And not one adult to keep an eye out for me. Home was just a place to grab food and to sleep. That was about it. Looking back at it now, though, I can understand that Mom's despair was exactly like mine, only I was a young and immature boy.

I took to hanging out on the streets and in the neighborhood pool hall. There, I met up with all kinds of people—mostly a lot of kids like me, from broken homes, who were always in trouble. Also with hoods, dope fiends, and derelicts. This dark subculture excited me. I listened to their crime stories and saw for myself how crooked the world was. As far as they were concerned, corruption was a way of life.

Right away, these guys were my role models and the guys I looked up to.

And in its own way, the people of this subculture took me under their wing. At fourteen, I met up with alcohol. Man, did it feel good going down, and as it numbed me up. But—man!—was it terrible coming back up. My first hangover was the worst thing I'd ever felt in my life. So why did I go back for more? Not like I was thinking about it!

Fourteen was the year I got busted for the first time. Grand theft, auto. Actually, I stole a couple of cars, purely for joy riding, before getting nailed. Because I was so young, I got away with seven months probation.

When I walked into the pool hall the next time, I was given a hero's welcome. "Hey, Tom—good job. You started your own rap sheet. Congratulations!"

Maybe that first crime was the one that marked me most. I was really *in.* I was an outlaw.

Fourteen was also the year I got into pills. Just sleeping pills at first. Then stronger barbiturates. It wasn't long before I was dissolving pills and shooting them into my veins. That was like getting hit with a club. To be honest, I'm not sure why I even liked that. Maybe because it made me just like everyone I hung out with. That, and it got me out of my head.

As if that wasn't enough, I got myself kicked out of the first of three high schools. I wasn't stupid, but I never applied myself. Trouble was also my middle name. I was *always* in trouble.

Mom would scream and yell at me. I'd yell right back in her face. Then I'd slam the door to my room and go to sleep, leaving her to drown her sorrows in a bottle of something. Who needed her anyway? I didn't need *anybody.*

As long as people just stayed off my back and out of my face, I could do just fine making my own way.

Something's Got Ahold of Me

When I woke up in a hospital bed, I had a moment of panic. Where was I? As my head cleared, it came back to me. I'd been shooting up pills, feeling the euphoria, then feeling myself being sucked down a spinning black hole of nausea.

I crawled up to a Catholic church. The priest put me in a cab, and took me to the hospital. The doctors said because I was too far gone and couldn't be saved, they wouldn't treat me. They only relented when the priest threatened to lay my dead body on the pavement and call the newspapers, telling them that a kid died because he'd been refused treatment.

Fortunately, the doctor got scared and told them to take me in. Later, I'd wonder if God had stepped in and saved my life.

After that I was sent to Boston State Hospital for observation. Sadly, my short stay in the state hospital accomplished nothing. Or almost nothing. One question I was asked by the doctors did make me think a little: Why was I doing drugs?

I never told them, but my secret answer was: *Because I hated the world and everyone in it.*

At fifteen, I knew in my gut that I was destined for some hard, hard times.

This was my world: Mom would come home from work and drink until the time she went to bed. We'd fight. She'd look at me with an empty hopelessness in her eyes. I couldn't stand that look. Sometimes I'd have to haul her upstairs to her bed. Sometimes I shut myself in my room, and we'd start the same mess over the next day. And sometimes I'd leave for days and go live with friends.

By now, at sixteen, I was committing multiple crimes every day. Breaking and entering. Robberies. Drug sales. When I wasn't in school—which was a lot of the time now—I was out on streets stealing and doping. Then I'd get busted and be sent to some juvenile facility.

As for my contact with Mom, all I can remember is screaming and shouting.

This was the year, 1966, when heroin seemed to take the streets of Boston by storm. It had been there for a long time—but before, it was associated with gutter bums and really hardcore users. Suddenly, it was the new drug of the new rock 'n' roll culture. Nice middle- and upper-class kids everywhere were shooting up. Everybody was doing some kind of drugs.

The first time I slipped a needle of heroin in my arm I knew I'd found what I needed to make my life work. This drug was *it* for me. To this day, I have no clue how I got through high school. I was high on something, or drinking heavily, every day. Just after I turned seventeen, I managed to graduate. But that's where the trail ended for me.

When I walked out the door of my high school for the last time, I felt both scared and excited. Now there was no one to tell me what to do, and I liked that. But I also had no career plan in mind. No future plans. Not a thing.

As I was becoming an adult, a new world was opening up to me. New people, nightclubs, all the different neighborhoods, and always breaking the law and in trouble.

WHO CARES?

Not that I spent a lot of time thinking about it. But in the rare moments when I thought about my life at all, it was with a shrug. *Who cares what I do with my life?* For the next two years, the only things I cared about were drugs and girls.

I got heavily into heroin. And to support my lifestyle, I also got heavily into committing crimes to get money for drugs.

Someone *did* care about my activities, however. That was the police and my parole officer. My probation was always extended because I was constantly in trouble. And so the next time I got busted, for possession of heroin at nineteen, I was in real trouble.

This time I was sent to a house of correction.

One year later, at the end of 1970, I was riding a bus in the old neighborhood. Re-entry to the free world was hard. Prison messes with your head. As I looked out the window, I reflected a little on the time behind bars. It was rough. Miserable. Mind numbing. Bad. *I am never going to get into a mess like this again,* I swore.

When the bus got to my stop, I stepped off thinking, *I'm through with drugs. I gotta find something to do with my life.*

"Hey, Tom!"

I turned my head. What a weird coincidence—there was Charlie, a guy who'd been one of my cellmates.

"Why don't you come over to my place?" he said, slapping me on the back. "I got a free one for you, to celebrate getting out."

In twenty minutes, I was wrapping a belt around my arm, thinking, *you're nuts. You've just been in prison for a year. You just promised yourself you'd go straight. And one little, stinking invitation undid the whole thing.*

But—I wanted that rush. Plunging the needle in a vein, I thought, *the heck with it.*

Within one day of getting out of prison, I was right back on heroin.

There was one thing that got me off drugs. I met an old girlfriend from high school. I wanted to get a job, settle down, go straight.

The thing was, I began to drink consistently. In fact, every day.

I was twenty-three when we got married. I was still on parole, of course, but I settled down, got a job, and became a decent guy. Without an education, and no union connections, there were no great jobs open to me. I found work in a machine shop in South Boston.

I found a job, but no real welcome. The old-timers were very secretive about their trade. When I'd walk over to a guy to ask a question, he'd put his tools down so I couldn't see how he was doing his work. No matter what question I asked, the answer was always some form of "Go figure it out for yourself, kid." No one was about to give me a break.

Even with nobody rooting for me, I began to want to do something with my life. I worked from 7 A.M. to 5 P.M. Then I left the shop and went straight to night school three evenings a week.

The thing was, though, it was a mind-numbing grind. In order to handle it, I drank every day after work. A little at first. Then heavily. An unbelievable amount of alcohol went through my body.

Four years into my marriage, I was drinking way, way too much—ignoring every one of my wife's pleas that I quit or at least slow down.

"It's not like I can't handle it," I told her, in defense. Alcohol got me through.

Then a business offer came my way.

One of my friend's brothers had his own business, making replacement moldings for auto bodies. He had a fantastic thing going on with car dealers and body shops all around Boston. I was a hard worker and a great asset to him.

While my buddy had a great thing going, he also had a problem. He was a degenerate gambler. When his creditors came after him, I wound up owning the business. Now, I didn't know a thing about operating a small business, but that didn't matter. His accountant took care of the books and kept me okay with the tax people. So suddenly I was flush with cash. With an adjustment here and there, and with three guys working for me, I was clearing $4,000 a month.

The drinking got to be too much now. I was drinking all day every day. But by now I knew I couldn't live straight. *Nobody lives without something,* I told myself. Not long after that, my old favorite, heroin, was back.

My wife was no fool. She knew the signs when she saw them. She begged. Then she threatened. It was no use. I was far more wedded to heroin than I was to her.

When she came across evidence that I was on dope again, she filed for divorce.

BANKRUPT

At least being married had given me some stability. Or maybe it was just someone to pretend for. With my wife gone, there was no longer a reason to keep up any kind of front. My drug use soared, and I began banging hundreds of dollars a day in all kinds of drugs.

With that kind of habit, I needed cash bad. After my own money was gone, I started working the banks. I got credit cards. Loans. The thing was, even as I sat there at another bank officer's desk, signing my name to yet another set of papers, I had no real thought of how I'd pay back a penny of all the cash I was carting away.

Needless to say, within a year's time I was a credit disaster. I'd burned everyone, and now they were screaming for their money.

One afternoon, I hauled two big shopping bags into the office of a Boston lawyer. It was eleven years after my prison jag. I'd built a life for myself—then lost it. I was just ripping people off for dope money again. As the lawyer watched, I dumped out the contents on his desk—bills from all my creditors. "I owe these people over $80,000," I complained. "You gotta help me out."

The guy looked at me like I was nuts. But there was money in it for him—$300 paid in cash (up front, of course). And when a judge discharged me of all debt, I thought I'd died and gone to heaven. Examining the papers, he said, simply, "I hereby declare you bankrupt." And that was it.

He had no idea how true that statement was.

To this day I can't think where the decision came from. I only remember there was a clear, conscious choice. Driving down the road, I faced this overwhelming sense that I was going nowhere. I'd always been heading nowhere. Why not just accept it?

A legitimate business had fallen in my lap. And I'd screwed it up. Pretty much, it was now dead. And from out of the blue, the words of a vow formed in my heart. I'm going to dedicate my life to doing drugs, and to crime. Maybe that was the road I was destined for.

About the same time, I ran into a friend of mine who had a blank prescription. I knew how to fill them out, and a plan came to me. My friend began stealing prescription pads. I would go to pharmacies and "cash in." Here was the plan. With stolen script pads in hand, we'd drive to drugstores all over New England and drive back to Boston with bottles and bottles of narcotics.

In my own head, I was "in business" again. To keep from getting caught, I started keeping detailed logbooks. What town and pharmacy I went to. What doctor's script pad I used. What pharmacist waited on me. What routes I took. No way was I going back to prison.

My whole life now centered around driving all over New England filling phony scripts. I'd lost the right to get a license at sixteen, got it back by crooked means for a short time—only to lose it again. So not only was I driving illegally, but I had to do it in hot cars.

If I'd spent half this much energy on building a legitimate business, I'd probably have been a millionaire. That thought never crossed my mind. And every ounce of energy went to running this scam, to satisfy one thing: My body craved several hundred dollars' worth of dope every day. The stuff I didn't use on myself I sold for more dope money.

And so I drove. And drove. And through the windows of my car, as the beauty of New England went by, I also saw young couples with their kids. Young men and women walking with their arms around each other. It was like another world. A kind of lifestyle I knew I'd never know.

This is my life, I'd think miserably. Driving. Stealing. Doping.

For a moment, maybe, thoughts of my dad would flit across my mind. But I'd lost him. Then lost Mom to alcohol. Then lost a wife. A business. Nothing I tried worked. And I was a stone-cold, "hope-to-die" dope fiend.

Somewhere along one of those picturesque New England roads, I threw in the towel on myself. Totally. How did I let myself get this morally bankrupt? How did I become so void of any concern for my self?

Because when I thought about myself and my future at all, that old voice inside would always ask, *who cares?*

Maybe Someone's Trying to Tell Me Something

From the get-go, I sensed something was funny.

I'd just handed a script to the guy behind the counter of a pharmacy in a little strip mall in Milford, Massachusetts. When he looked at it, there was a second's hesitation. When he looked up at me, something in his eyes had changed.

"I'm a little busy, so it'll be a few minutes," he said. "You can look around the store while I fill this for you."

"I've got another errand. I'll be back," I said casually.

Back in the car, I drove a few blocks away. Found a pay phone. Waited a little while. Phoning the pharmacy, I identified myself by the fake name on the prescription and asked if it was ready. There was a slight hesitation in the young woman's voice. Then—"Uh, yeah. You can come and get it now."

When I pulled into the parking lot, everything looked quiet. All I noticed was a kid heading into the pharmacy. "Hey, kid… Come here," I called.

He came to the car window, and I held up twenty dollars. "I just got my leg out of a cast and I can't walk. Here's a tip for you, if you'll go and pick up my prescription for me."

He wasn't in the store more than two minutes, when I saw him come back to the front door with the store manager—and he pointed out my car.

At the same moment, down at the far end of the strip mall, I saw movement. An unmarked police car was nosing out from hiding.

My foot slammed on the gas pedal, and I was gone.

Three police cars pulled in line behind me, as I ran red lights and jumped sidewalks, blasting my way out of town.

Only one thought possessed me as I sped like a madman out through the country. *They're gonna have to kill me because I'm not going back to jail.*

The other thought I had was to get rid of the pills, and I began eating as many as I could. In short order, I passed through a couple more towns, not slowing one bit. In each town a couple more cop cars joined the chase. Pretty soon I could count the red-flashing lights of fifteen or more cruisers in my rearview mirror.

Suddenly, one of the cruisers pulled out of the line and sped up till it was right beside me. I was about to look over at the officer—when he turned his car into mine. The jolt knocked me, and my right tires dropped off the edge of the road, spitting gravel. I jammed the wheel to the left, and jerked the wheels back onto the roadway.

The cruiser was still keeping pace, and it was probably only a matter of seconds before he tried to slam me again. But I beat him to it. Jerking my wheel to left, I slammed hard into his passenger side.

The jolt, the sound of screeching metal on metal, was incredible. It sent the cruiser veering to the left—and off into a ditch.

In my mirror I could see the lead car speed up, pulling up fast behind me. *Is this guy gonna be stupid enough to try it, too. Didn't he see what I just did to the other guy…?*

At that moment I crested a hill, and when I dropped my eyes from the rearview mirror, I saw—too late—the sharp right turn I was into. A shock of terror bolted through me, and I spun the wheel. But it was too late. Dead ahead was a huge tree—and then came the crash of metal and the flying glass.

How I survived the crash, I don't know. The next thing I knew, I was surrounded by police who flung open the car door and dragged me out onto the ground.

Dazed from the pills and the crash I looked up into the ring of angry faces and police revolvers surrounding me. "*Shoot me,*" I shouted. "Pull the trigger! Kill me! Just *do* it!"

The officers looked at me like I was nuts—like I was just daring them. But I meant it. At that moment, I wanted nothing so much as I wanted to die.

I was not lucky enough, of course, to get my wish. Instead, the charges against me were not only narcotics violations but also the attempted murder of a police officer with a motor vehicle.

My partner raised $5,000 for my bail—and even then, when I got out, I got arrested *again* on new charges. Now it really was the end of the road.

Although I was facing years in prison, some type of amazing grace started to intervene. I called Jack, my ex-brother-in-law, who was an old friend and now a cop. He picked me up and got me home in one piece. He helped me find a drug program to go into.

I had amassed over two hundred charges in five different courts. That's why it seemed like a true miracle—my lawyer was stunned—when the judges thought they saw some redeemable possibility for my life. They announced that they were going to allow me to go into a "hardcore drug program" instead of life in Walpole State Prison as a habitual offender.

The Third Nail was a therapeutic community—a lot like boot camp.

They took away everything. Shaved your head. I know the intent was good. They wanted to break you down. Get you past all your defenses. Then their counselors could rebuild you. I knew this was the routine, and so it didn't have much effect on me. Besides, I was long past caring about anything. Inside I *knew* I was going to be a hopeless drug addict all my life.

My life was so chaotic that an NBC-TV affiliate actually did a short documentary on me—to illustrate how drugs mess up lives—which was narrated by Dan Travanti of *Hill Street Blues.* What a sad way, I thought, to memorialize your life.

It was during my time at The Third Nail that an ex-addict and his family came to talk to us from a group called Teen Challenge. As I sank into my seat to hear the guy talk, I was surprised to see the black book he was holding in one hand.

A Bible? I thought. Somebody snickered. *Oh no, we're in for a religious lecture.* But I was curious. No one had ever in my whole life talked to me from the Bible.

From his first words, I was intrigued.

"Jesus is alive today," he said. "Do you know that?"

By this point, I probably hadn't set foot in a church in more than twenty years. In the back of my head, though, I did believe in God. And

I guess I believed in Jesus Christ, too. But it had never occurred to me that if Jesus was God, then He was alive *today.*

"He knows all about what's been going on in your life," the speaker went on. "And He cares about you."

God cares about me? I'd never heard this kind of talk before. It sounded strange. Not like I spent time crying about it, but *nobody* cared about me. I didn't even care about myself.

But something in the guy's words shot right into a deep place inside me.

"God knows all your lying. Your stealing. Your illegal doping," he said. "And He *still* cares about you. That's why He died to pay the price for your sins."

Every Friday, the same guy came back to talk to us from the Bible. He was the only real, live, active Christian I'd ever met in my life. I didn't think they existed in this day and age.

And with everything the guy said, it was like a message was coming clear. Everything I'd tried hadn't worked. Maybe it was because I messed up. But *maybe* it was also because I'd been trying to go in wrong directions all my life and I was being prevented from going that way—and *maybe* someone was trying to tell me something.

For the first time in my life since Dad died, I opened up to the possibility: Maybe someone did care about me after all.

Finally, after months of his visits, I bowed my head at the end of his talk, and prayed. *God, I need your help.*

It was all I could think to say.

That's all that was needed.

Slow Change

I've heard people talk about "turning their life over to God." Usually, it kind of sounds like they went from being Jesse James to being like an apostle overnight.

That definitely wasn't the case for me.

When I finished the program at The Third Nail, in 1982, I was still at a loss about what I should do with my life. No angel voices told me what to do. And I sure had no interest in church. Period.

I was determined not to deal drugs, though. And fortunately I heard they were hiring at a local state school. Fernald was an institution for the developmentally disabled. The only opening they had was in the only building on their grounds that had locked wards. I took it, not knowing what I was in for.

The guys on this ward were in their twenties and thirties and seriously developmentally delayed. Their emotional state was so severe that they easily became violent. Not only did they assault each other, they assaulted the workers, too.

When I realized what the job was about, I thought that maybe a "nut" like me could help these people. And, I'd be a state worker. I'd be legitimate, on my way to some kind of success.

Immediately, I found I could work with them. Something in me opened up and connected with these guys. The thought wasn't uppermost in my head, but they were like me in a way. They were largely forgotten. Disenfranchised. Who came to see them? *No one.* Who even cared they existed? *No one.*

But I cared. I didn't really know *why* I cared. Almost at once, though, I found myself getting attached to these guys inside the locked ward. And as the weeks passed, I found myself looking forward to seeing them every morning, even looking forward to going to work! Maybe it was the first time since Dad died I'd ever really cared about somebody, the first time I felt like I belonged to something worthwhile. When Mom shut me out with her drinking, I'd shut her out. Maybe it was because I cared about somebody *else* again that it felt like *my* life mattered.

As these changes took place in me slowly, I actually came to love these guys. Work was very hard. Once I saw a guy get so angry that he ripped a bumper off a car—the rage gave him *that* kind of superhuman strength. And yet, in our good moments, we had a ball.

As I said, though, my life was no miracle-transformation story. When I'd first gotten out of Third Nail, I was sober as a judge. Not doping. Not drinking. But sure enough, the old attitude came back.

When I was tense or tired, I heard that little voice that said, *you gotta have* something. I began to smoke pot regularly. Then I'd sell a little, just to have enough to buy a small bag.

For three years, that was my life. Go to work. Come home and smoke a lot of pot. Deal a little. I met this girl and that girl. I got an apartment and a car. In a year, I was in line to become a supervisor. I did so well with these difficult guys, there was talk of sending me to college to get better trained.

By the end of 1982, though, something was troubling me. I knew that just smoking pot wasn't going to last—pretty soon I'd be back on the hardcore stuff if I kept going this way. I kept going back to that time I'd asked God to help me. I knew God was there somewhere in my life. And yet—was *this* what God wanted me to do with my life?

Why did I have the feeling there was something else? And if there was—how would I ever figure out what it was?

Strangely enough, I was rolling out of bed on a cold, clear day in January in 1984 when something inside me just crumbled. I sank down on my knees beside the bed. And these words came out of me, from someplace deep inside.

"I'm done, God," I prayed. "I'm done fighting you. I don't know what you want to do with me. If you want me to become religious or whatever, and wear a robe or something, whatever it is. Anything. Take my life—*all* of it—and do something with it."

When the rush of words was over, I shook my head. *Wow. What was that about?* Then I started to get up off my knees when something started coming over me.

I'd never felt anything like this before. The bedroom was exactly the same, of course. But inside me, it was like a door I wasn't aware of had opened up wide. I truly felt God telling me, *don't worry, kid. Everything is going to be all right. Don't be afraid of how I'm going to do it, but I'm going to give you a whole new life.*

LIFE MATTERS

Finally, I put all the drugs down for good.

My whole outlook on life changed immediately.

At work, I scared myself a little. I found myself walking up to people and just saying—in fact, blurting out—stuff like, "Guess what! I'm gonna be a Christian." I still had no idea what this meant.

Mainly, the people at work looked at me like I was crazy. If I was in their shoes I would have, too.

It was during that time that I called Pete, the guy who'd come to minister to me at The Third Nail.

Pete and his wife invited me to come and live with them in Roxbury. These people lived very humbly, and when Pete wasn't working, he spent all his time talking to people about God. Getting them to go to church.

"Tell me what to do to be a Christian," I asked him.

In response, Pete and his wife let me move in with them and their family. If ever I needed evidence that God cared for His own, it came to me through these people. Their kindness and generosity, not to mention the intensity of their faith, were like nothing I'd ever experienced in my life.

Still, there was the question: *If my life does matter, what am I going to do with it?*

One evening, in the middle of a discussion, I laid it on Pete. "Okay, I'm thirty-three years old. What am I going to do with my life now?"

Pete scratched his chin. "What do you *want* to do?" Pete firmly believed that God was like a good human father—in the sense that He was the one who put desires in our hearts and then went about the business of helping us fulfill them.

I let out a long breath. I couldn't help thinking that I wanted to help people find their way out of the insanity of messed up lives, the way God was helping me find my way out.

"You know," I said, "I got a lot of help at that drug rehab program I was in. But someone should have a program like that, and make it *Christian.*"

Pete's face looked like the sun was slowly rising in it. "Someone *does* have programs like that," he said.

"You're kidding?"

"It's called Teen Challenge."

This is the kind of guy Pete was. It wasn't enough just to *tell* me about Teen Challenge. Or to tell me where there was a Teen Challenge center and send me to visit it. Pete prayed and believed God had an idea for us to pursue.

We started in Massachusetts and headed south. Pete's plan was to take me to Teen Challenge centers all down the East Coast. "We'll just trust God to direct us," he said. "We'll go wherever someone will let me talk about God's ability to set people free. And then you can tell how God has freed you from a whole lifetime of drug addiction."

With the same enthusiasm I threw into pursuing drugs, I now began to pursue a new life.

What followed was nothing less than six months of small but sure miracles.

Pete would pull up to a Teen Challenge center—say, in New York or Philadelphia—and tell them we wanted to talk about deliverance from drug addiction. And the next thing we knew, he was speaking from the Bible to a roomful of guys, followed up by me telling my story. I should say, telling the story of how God reached down to a guy who had stopped caring about his own life.

Always, our talks were followed by an invitation—to a meal, a place to spend a night or two, or to speak at local church. I began to believe that God was taking care of us.

But as we neared Georgia, the southernmost point and the end of our trip, one big question haunted me. What was I going to do with my life? *This?* Travel around the country and just expect people to take me in and feed me?

One morning, reading my Bible, I felt like something Jesus told a crowd of anxious people was directed right to me. Personally. He told them:

> ...do not worry about your life, what you will eat or drink; or about your body, what you will wear. Is not life more important than food, and the body more important than clothes?

> Look at the birds of the air; they do not sow or reap or store away in barns, and yet your heavenly father feeds them…

And as I continued to read this passage, these words in particular leaped off the page at me:

> Are you not much more valuable than they?… So do not worry…. Seek first God's kingdom and his righteousness…
> (MATTHEW 6:25-26, 31, 33)

It hit me then. Tears filled my eyes.

When my dad died—and even before then—I'd had *another* father standing in the wings, ready to look out for me and help me through life. No one had ever told me that, though. And so I'd made my own way. And as it turned out, it was the *wrong* way. Big time.

Now, through every little miracle of help and provision I was witnessing on this trip, and through these words from the Bible, God seemed to say to me, *Let me be your Dad, and you won't ever have to feel like you're on your own again. Just look for the way to work alongside me in the work I'm doing, setting people free inside the way you're now free. And I'll take care of all the anxieties you used to shoulder when you believed you were totally on your own in the world. That's how your life is going to work.*

Back in Boston a few days later, it was the end of the road. I wondered, *what am I going to do?*

The string of events that followed, like some kind of divine clockwork, was remarkable. The details are important only to me.

In a nutshell, through Pete, I met a guy who was heading, of all things, to a *Teen Challenge* program in Boston. He believed I was one more guy sent to them by God to help their team in the work of bringing God's grace to other recovering addicts. And that's not all. Not by far.

In the sixteen years since I began working with Teen Challenge, I can tell you that my life has not all been easy. But it has most definitely been *blessed!* I've been blessed with personal miracles—such as Shirley, my new wife, life partner, *and* best friend. Blessed with daily miracles at work—like seeing funds come in at times when needs in the program are critical. Also blessed with seeing other lives change miraculously right before my eyes.

Most of all, I've been blessed every day of my life knowing this: I once was a kid who lost his dad, and then lost his way. I grew to be a man who believed no one cared about me—so why should I care about anyone? Or even care about myself?

Once, I was alone and destined to a life of failure.

Today, I know I have a God and Father who asks each one of us to trust our lives into His hands. He asks us to do that because He can care for us much better than we can care for ourselves. His plan for our life may be different than the one we would have chosen. But if we turn our lives over to His care, we'll begin to see the wonders of His workings on the new path He opens up for us.

Trust it! And you will see it happen!

INSIGHT FOR US ALL

Rev. Tom Parker is now the Director of Administration for Teen Challenge New England. He attended Bible college, and has worked toward his master's degree in counseling. For a guy who'd given up on himself, he's one of the most responsible and hopeful guys you'd ever want to meet.

What we can learn from Tom's story speaks to us all.

Primarily, we see the turmoil someone goes through when he has no plan or goal for the future. Tom was a young man who had no guidance, no direction. In that vacuum of meaninglessness, the haze and numbness of drugs became an easy escape. And once he made his way into that lifestyle, the temptation to make cash the "easy" way proved too great.

Underneath it all, Tom carried a sense that if no one really cared about him, why should he care about himself? When you have a low sense of self-worth, your reasoning tells you, *I might as well be a criminal as anything else. If I'm not important, what does it matter?*

Low self-esteem is one of the main reasons young people get involved in illicit sex, drinking, and drugs. And of course it's the greatest contributing factor to teenage suicide—even the long, slow kind, like addiction.

If you're a parent, one of the greatest things you can do is to help your child develop a vision of himself or herself for the future.

If you're a person who's into drugs now, stop and ask yourself, "Is this the way I want my life to go? From one hit, one party, to the next?"

Maybe something in your life has given you the message that you aren't worth very much—so why does it matter *what* you're into? If so, you need to seek out a Christian counselor, perhaps through one of the Teen Challenge centers. A wise and godly counselor can help you find the path that God has set for you. They can help you come out of the mind-clouds of hopelessness that drugs bring, and help you step into clear-thinking reality again.

Don't go one more day believing that you've blown your chance at a great life. Teen Challenge is all about the work of helping people realize that the God who is father to us all *cares.* Because of that fact, we can start to care about ourselves.

Speaking of clouded thinking, a second lesson we learn from Tom's story is how badly drug use warps our thought processes. In particular, Tom got involved in a scam, writing fake prescriptions. Not only that, but he justified his scam, telling himself that he wasn't really hurting anyone. After all, he was only taking a few pills here and there from pharmacies. In his way of thinking, no one was really hurt. After all, these were chain stores, and what did the loss of a few pills matter? Besides, he was paying for them.

But the fact is, scams like Tom's—not to mention outright thefts—are costing businesses millions and millions in losses every year. The drug culture contributes to this major offense against honest businesspeople, because so many drug users involve themselves in scams great and small as a way to come up with money to support their habits.

If you're involved in a scam, don't cloud the issue by telling yourself, "At least I'm not into violent crimes." Straighten out your thinking on this one. You don't have to be into violent crime to *be* a criminal. And if you're squeezing or manipulating money from your family or friends for drugs, you *are* scamming money from them for illicit and illegal uses.

Third—and this is sad to say—the man from Teen Challenge who Tom met while in the rehab program was the first live, active Christian he'd ever met in his life. It was through this man that Tom experienced the care and concern of God himself for the very first time.

If you're a Christian reading this, *think about it.*

Sometimes those of us who are firmly entrenched in churches forget there's a whole world full of guys like Tom, and also many women in need. They've never heard the Bible read. They've never been told God is real, and that He has the power to change their lives—not only the power but the desire, too!

Is there a Christian outreach program that needs your support? *You bet.* Are there people who need to know God cares about them, no matter how hurt, confused, or messed up their lives are right now? *Yes, there are.* Do programs like Teen Challenge need your volunteer help, your financial support, and your prayers? *Indeed they do!*

There are two mistakes I can make at this point. One is to push you too hard to get involved in some way in a program like Teen Challenge. The other is not to push you at all. Brothers and sisters in Christ, concerned businesspeople: *We can make a difference!*

Don't hold back any longer, believing the lie that society is just going down the tubes, and there's nothing we can do about it. Our efforts, our finances, and our prayers can make a huge difference in *someone's* life.

Your touch, your giving, your words may make all the difference to someone, like Tom, who never believed that anyone cared.

As we've seen already, Tom's belief from childhood was that nobody really cared about him. I want to return to that, because there's one more important lesson here.

When you think no one cares about you, you stop caring about other people. It's like a wall of defense. ("If you don't care about me, I won't care about you.") Not caring is a way to strike back.

The problem is, in the end, the bitterness you carry also causes you to stop caring about *yourself*. So in the end, the one you're hurting most is you.

Tom's recovery from drug addiction did involve a miraculous moment when God seemed to intervene and take away his desire for drugs, and also nicotine and alcohol. But along with that, we need to recognize that something else helped him stay clean of addictive substances. That's the fact that Tom learned to stop focusing entirely on himself and began to focus on giving out to someone besides himself.

What problem are you dealing with in your life? Is there some wound from the past that just won't seem to go away? God seems to have set up a system here. The way it works is this:

As we give to others, we begin to experience healing and blessing ourselves, and freedom from the wounds of the past.

Today, ask God to lift your eyes off the problems and wounds you may be carrying. Ask Him to show you, as I said above, who you can go to for a healing touch of concern.

And then be ready to experience in your own life the blessing of healing and new freedom that comes back to you.

CHAPTER SIX

"HOPE...AND A FUTURE"

— Rodney Hart —

One of the saddest things about the drug culture is that it wastes lives.

How many young people start out with great potential—and then get involved with "recreational" drug use and watch their lives go down the tubes? There is no way to know. Drug use is as devastating as the proverbial plague of locusts. The waste of talent and creative imagination is utterly tragic.

A recent *Time* magazine article, in fact, reported that the new craze drug, ecstasy, "resculpts the brain." Researchers at Johns Hopkins tested ecstasy users and found that their brain functioning abilities were "far worse" than control groups that did not use drugs. These specialists have concluded that "changes to [brain] cells [in people using ecstasy] are permanent" and that "the damage is irreversible." And ecstasy is certainly not the only drug that's been shown to permanently alter or damage the minds of its users.

Is there a way to rescue the minds and talents that are being lost to us? Can anything turn around a life that's headed for a dead end?

If anyone's life holds the answers to those questions, it's Rodney Hart's life.

◆ ◆ ◆

MEET RODNEY HART

All I had to do was to think of my grandfather, and my chest would stick out with pride.

Grandpa had been a silver medalist in hockey in the very first winter Olympics, in 1924. Not only that, he'd also been a player for the Montreal Canadiens. Sure, he'd been a rascal, and abandoned my grandmother when Mom was just a little girl. But that didn't register much with a little boy like me who had a heart full of athletic dreams and ambitions. He was my hero!

Not that my own dad was a slouch. I admired him, too, but for other reasons. My dad was the hardest working guy I knew. He drove a truck for Nabisco, delivering cookies all week. Then drove a cab on weekends. Mom worked, too, as a nurse. And they put in all this effort so we could live in the upscale Boston neighborhood of Newton. Okay, so we were definitely working class and ours was not exactly one of the better houses. No matter. My folks were an example of what hard work and determination could do for you.

It was Grandpa's silver medal in the Olympics that gave me bragging rights, though. As a little kid, I'd skate the frozen ponds of our neighborhood with the roar of imaginary crowds in my head. And the rest of the year, say, when I was playing Pop Warner football, I played with so much drive and energy that the league let me play above my age group, on a team that won the state championship.

I always had the sense my parents were proud of us kids, too. I say us, because I had two older brothers and one older sister whom they "raised right." That's what I'd overhear people say about us. Because the Hart kids were never in trouble.

Not until one stray remark changed everything for me.

"YOU WERE AN ACCIDENT"

It's odd how a tiny incident can redirect your life.

I was ten, and hanging out at the local playground with a bunch of friends. One kid had been looking at me funny, and finally just blurted out, "You were an accident."

The other kids were suddenly quiet. I had no clue what he meant. "You're crazy."

"No, I'm not," he went on. "I heard my parents talking. You were an *accident.* So that means your parents never wanted to have you."

We were all just figuring out what sex was about, and it dawned on me what he was saying. It must have hit the other guys, too, because a couple of them started laughing and taunting. "Ooo...! Your parents were messing around. And out came little Rodney."

"Shut up, you idiots," I said. But my face was hot with embarrassment. I couldn't let them know what was going on inside me.

I was an accident.

Mercifully, somebody changed the subject. But mentally, I was in a different place. This piece of news had landed in me like a drill bit, boring its message down into me: *My parents had wanted my brothers and sisters. They didn't want me.*

For days, this painful thought was fresh in my mind. The more I turned it over in my head, the more I knew the kid had to be right. Dad was sixty.

A really big change went on inside me.

I'd always been aggressive in sports. The one thing you could always count on was that whenever I threw myself into something, I did it whole-hog. And now I got really tough. On the football field, when I played linebacker on defense, if someone got in my way, I'd go for blood.

I was going to prove to the world I was no accident. I was *somebody.*

TROUBLE

Living in the affluent neighborhood of Newton forced me to see the financial discrepancies between me and a lot of my neighbors and classmates. Whereas people in some parts of Newton owned their own businesses and lived in very nice homes, my folks were holding on by their fingernails and our house was older. Other kids played in the hockey leagues, but the equipment and fees were too expensive for my folks. So for me it was pickup hockey on a frozen swamp, or nothing.

My aggression increased. Now I started getting into fights.

I also started getting into alcohol. There had always been alcohol around our house. When Dad asked me to get him beer, I'd fish one out of the fridge, pop it open for him... and then take a swig before delivering it. Then there were the shot glasses of Manischewitz wine my grandmother offered me.

What my parents never suspected was this: Right under their noses I was developing a taste and a craving for alcohol. Their eleven-year-old kid loved the buzz! Alcohol made me feel like a big man. Reckless.

It was the same feeling I got when I watched my favorite TV show, a mid-1960s potboiler called "It Takes a Thief." It was about a high-class "cat burglar" who would have been considered nothing but jailbait, except the government pulled him out of jail to pull off risky heists for them. His ability to pull off burglaries against the most sophisticated defenses and impossible odds was his mark of distinction. He was a class act.

That's what I wanted to be. A class act. I wasn't going to achieve recognition in school, that was for sure. Books and tests were a total bore. Getting by with Cs and Ds was okay by me. But the idea of pulling off some "heists"—now that had possibilities! *Outlaw.* That's how I'd make my mark.

It was a cold winter afternoon, and a gang of us headed out with skates and hockey sticks over our shoulders to play "swamp hockey" on the frozen pond behind the graveyard. As we walked through the neighborhood, though, I noticed that someone had left their garage door open a bit. Inside were some six-packs of Miller beer.

That afternoon, I sat the guys down and drew out a plan on a piece of paper. And that evening, we broke in and stole the beer. It wasn't the first time I'd gotten drunk. But at eleven, I'd made my first successful step toward my chosen "career"—which was "professional thief."

From that day on, I stole everything I could get my hands on. The kids who came from better-off families had mini-bikes. When I found out where one was sitting in a garage a few blocks away, I broke the lock one night and stole it. Since we had a hideout down by the swamp, too, I hid it there. And after I'd used it a while, I sold it.

In no time at all, I got bold about my "heists." I'd go into a store, for instance, and get the clerk to start showing me something out of a jewelry case—maybe a watch. I could tell pretty quickly if the clerk was on the ball or not. We'd get quite a few watches out, and I'd then I'd get them to put one or two back and take three others out. While they reached into another part of the case for what I wanted, I'd slip a watch in my pocket.

When I was in the seventh grade, one of my friends took me out behind the junior high school to show me a joint he'd stolen from his older brother. It was 1970, and drugs had been flowing freely around our neighborhood for some time.

"You want to smoke this with me?" he offered.

In a few minutes, we were both in a haze.

From that day on, true to form, I threw myself into smoking dope. Besides making my mark as a thief, I became a pothead. At fifteen dollars an ounce, four or five of us would buy an ounce and smoke it all. Then go down to Burger King and eat four Whoppers.

Not long after, my curiosity about other drugs moved me on to try speed and crystal meth. That got old and I added LSD. Older kids in the neighborhood supplied me, and by fourteen, I was smoking and doing some kind of pills every day.

Over time, my petty heists also got boring. Fourteen was the year I decided to take it to the next level.

Not too far away was a cab station. One evening, after dark, I walked nonchalantly past the lot. A couple guys were standing outside the office door, smoking. When they went inside, I quickly walked up to the line of empty cabs at the edge of the lot. Just as I'd heard, they were all unlocked, with keys in them.

And so the first time I drove a car, it was a stolen cab. My friends were wide-eyed with disbelief when I drove up. "You're *nuts,* man." "You idiot." But everyone piled in, and we had a ball until the gas ran out.

Now I was the *man!* If there wasn't any trouble to get into, I'd make some. For the next year and a half, whenever someone said, "Hey, Rodney, go steal a car," I was there.

The crazy thing was, the guys at the cabstand didn't seem to learn.

Gratefully Dead in the Head

The only thing I can figure about my parents during this time is that they were probably tired out from raising three kids before me. That, and they still worked killer hours. The bottom line was, they weren't really aware of what was going on with me.

The few times they did get a glimpse into my life, they didn't react very strongly.

For instance, I'd begun keeping quantities of pot in a dresser drawer. A friend who had a greenhouse full of it supplied me. My grandmother, who lived with us, came across it one day putting clean clothes away. When my parents found out, they just shrugged it off. Their attitude seemed to be, "We smoked cigarettes in our day. So all these kids are smoking pot—it's not that bad."

I liked that "laid-back" attitude! It was kind of like the philosophy I'd picked up from the Grateful Dead. Just smoke up and let it all *be.*

Still, nobody's parents were into letting us party. So on weekends we smoked and drank—and started making out with girls—in local playgrounds. Even in the graveyard. And all during the week, we joked about going to "get high school," since all we did was... well, get high.

Though I didn't see it at the time, something in me began to change. I dropped out of sports. If I thought about it at all, I chalked it up to the hippie ethos of the times. But it was something deeper than that. As a little kid, I'd envisioned myself as a professional athlete, just like my grandfather. Now, when I thought about sports at all, it was just not me. It was work. I wasn't *into* working now.

With that deep change in attitude, any sense of direction or purpose I'd had blew away in marijuana smoke. I was happy to get high all the time, and to face life dead in the head.

There was one slight problem with my philosophy. Money for drugs had to come from somewhere.

When I graduated high school in 1974, way near the bottom of my class, not a day went by that I didn't wake up and reach for a joint or some pills. Since my parents were out the door to work long before my eyes were open, no one knew what I was up to right there in my room.

With this do-nothing attitude, where was drug money going to come from?

After high school, I got a full-time job with a landscaping company. The owners were party animals. My kind of people. It wasn't a great-paying job, but as it turned out, the people who hired us to care for their property generally had the better homes and higher incomes. So while I was busy trimming their hedges or mowing, I'd scope out each house.

After dark, I started my other "job." Returning to one of the homes where we'd worked, I'd break in and rifle the place for cash. The thing is, people were crazy and very predictable. There'd always be cash in a top drawer, or under a mattress, in obvious places. Churches were also a great target because some pastor or secretary would usually leave collection money lying in a drawer.

I stole for the drug money. My goal was to keep my head as dead as could be. And to be honest, I also stole just for the thrill of it.

DESTRUCTIVE STREAK

Other changes began to happen.

My moods began to swing. Instead of being a laid-back pothead, I became very cocky and arrogant. Probably this was the result of all the speed I was doing. Very quickly I became more aggressive and began picking fights all the time.

On top of that, I developed a destructive streak. A dangerous one.

I blow-torched a person's basement. Along with some friends, I broke into a school building and wrecked the place. We'd steal gasoline out of people's garages, dump it in the street, and light it on fire. We'd go up to a wealthy area of Newton and place small explosives, called M-80s, against people's picture windows and blow them out.

Amazingly, no one ever got hurt. And I got off on the destruction left in my wake.

The crazier things got, the closer I got to self-destruction.

It was January 1973, and I'd just turned sixteen. We'd been partying for two days, when a bunch of us heard there was a big party happening on the other side of the city. PCP had just hit the streets, along with synthetic THC. Maybe we could score some. "Come on, Rodney," someone said, "steal a car." That's all I needed to hear.

I stole a Buick station wagon with a 427 engine. Man, did that thing haul!

The car was great; the party stunk.

We left, and drove all around the city and surrounding towns. We were getting higher by the minute, singing at the top of our lungs to rock music on the radio as we blasted around the midnight streets.

"Come on, Rodney," said my friend, who we called "Mouse." "Let me drive."

We were in the town of Waltham, and I was tired of driving now. On the other hand, Mouse had never driven in his life. This could be wild.

I pulled over and we switched places. Mouse had just taken the wheel when Deep Purple's monster hit, "Smoke On the Water," came on.

Mouse's head snapped around, and he had a wild look in his eyes. Then he stomped on the gas. Tires burning on pavement, he swerved out into the street right into oncoming traffic.

"You stupid…" I began shouting at Mouse. He veered left, directly in front of another car. I grabbed for the wheel—but too late.

The telephone pole was dead center, coming at us.

The next thing I knew, I was waking up. Someone was handcuffing me to the car. My head ached and was covered in glass from the broken windshield. The fact that I was wearing a hat probably saved me from getting my head and face slashed up. I felt like vomiting.

Mouse and the others were gone. "Your buddies ran off and left you," said the guy handcuffing me. Then he identified himself as a police officer. He'd been off duty when we nearly front-ended him.

When the case came to juvenile court, Mouse ratted. I was the fall guy. The judge gave me a year on probation.

On the drive home, Dad silent and unhappy in the front seat, I was thinking, *how in the world am I going to stay out of trouble for a year? I'm going to wind up in reform school.* It dawned on me that something might really be wrong inside my head. All I thought about was drugs and stealing.

For some reason, it never occurred to me to stop doing drugs. I *loved* drugs. I loved the vandalism. I have no clue why.

My year of probation was far from over when I wrecked another stolen car. This time I broke my wrist and some ribs. Another guy with me almost lost an eye. This time, my cousin, who was a Newton police officer, happened to get to the scene and he let us run.

I lied to my parents about the broken bones. One more lie hardly mattered. I lied now even when I didn't have to lie.

Shortly after that, I was caught selling drugs in a men's room at a Catholic school dance. The cops who got me took the drugs, then let me go because they knew my cousin.

By now I was convinced. *Something really is wrong with my head. I can't even control myself anymore. I'm not going to do this anymore.*

Cleaning Up

These last two close calls convinced me I had to clean up my act. I felt motivated, and confident I could do it. I got myself into the Outward Bound program at school. A couple of us were juvenile delinquents, while the rest were straight kids.

The program was going to take us up to Mt. Washington, the highest peak in New England, for a winter campout. That meant we had to start training and get into shape. Life in a tent on a frozen mountain, not to mention the hike up, would be a huge challenge.

Amazingly, I stopped drinking. Pot was still an everyday thing and no big deal. I planned to do pot my whole life!

And then…

Somebody—probably me—got the great idea to bust into a dorm at a local private school while the kids were home on winter break. No doubt, we'd turn up cash, maybe drugs. Right in mid-heist, someone looked out a window. "Police cruisers! They know we're here."

Escape meant jumping out a second story window. The jump went great. The landing was terrible. That night I limped home on a badly sprained ankle. The Outward Bound trip was over. As I lay on my bed that night, I gave up. *Here I am again. I said I wasn't going to do this any-*

more. I said I was going to clean up. There was no way. Shortly after, I quit the program. I'd have to reform myself—later.

After graduation in 1974, I went back to my reliable, standby job with the landscaping company. I worked days, and partied every evening and weekend. Somewhere in the back of my head, even after my failure, I stubbornly held onto the conviction that I *could* clean myself up one of these days, when I really wanted to.

But that fall, when the outdoor work season ended, my drug use went off the scale. Mom and Dad went off to work, faithful as clockwork. And I lay around, collecting unemployment and getting seriously stoned from morning till night.

The truth was way too plain to miss anymore. My parents now knew their youngest son was a dope fiend. They just didn't have a clue what to do about it. We came to an impasse, because they didn't want to encourage me in the lifestyle I was living and I was far from ready to go straight. When they decided to move from Newton to a mobile home outside the city, I stuffed clothes in a sack and took off on my own.

In a few days, I was a dirty street bum, with filthy clothes and long, matted, greasy hair.

So much for my attempts at cleaning up.

Reality Breaks Apart

I can only piece together images—like snapshots and film clips from my memory—about what happened in the next few months. Reality was breaking up.

When I walked out of my parents' house in Newton, I was literally out on the streets. It was spring, and very cold at night in Boston. At first I went and slept in Kenmore station near Fenway Park. Or I'd sleep on benches on Boston Common, or in subway stations. For a short time I stayed with a friend. Then I met a girl, and spent nights at her place.

The problem with staying with people was this: They'd take me in out of generosity, and I'd rip them off for dope money and disappear. Half my head would say, *what the heck are you doing?* But I was getting more out of control every day.

Very quickly, I became "mud" even to my friends.

Between the doping and my nomadic lifestyle, I got pretty wild looking. My weight dropped. My hair hung down my back in long braids. Days were spent doping. In the morning, I'd drop acid. In the afternoon, it was crystal meth or mushrooms. At night, I got drunk.

So much for all those good intentions about "cleaning up" my life. I was homeless, dirty, and now I also became delusional.

I thought that when people died, they became an energy that shot out into the universe, and they became stars. I'd also read a biography of Geronimo and believed that I could invite his spirit to possess me, so I did. Now I walked around imagining that this long-dead Indian warrior's spirit inhabited me.

My father found me on the streets. The look on his face was desperate. He hadn't seen me in weeks. "You look like the devil," he told me.

After that, a plan emerged. My brother Glenn, who'd just gotten married, needed some help.

"I just got a place on Cape Cod and we're moving," Glenn told me when I saw him again. "Come live with us for a while. You'll get a break from all this,"—meaning the drugs and park benches—"and you can get your stuff together. It'll be great. Come on. Help me move."

"Help" isn't a word I'd use.

I showed up late—when the truck was packed and they were ready to leave. Given my drug-fried look and dirty appearance, my sister-in-law had a fearful look in her eyes. Glenn cornered me. "Look, I gotta lay down a condition. You're squirrelly. All this crazy Geronimo talk. We can find a psychiatrist to treat you. So you can come and stay *if* you promise to let us help."

"Sure," I shrugged.

That night, after my brother and his wife had fallen into an exhausted sleep, I was still up. I'd been no help at all. And now a new idea was buzzing in my head. *Steal the rental truck.*

Somehow, I made my way through the dark streets. The drugs I'd been taking all day had me out of my mind, and I was thinking, *I'll just park this baby in the woods somewhere and live out of it. Me and Geronimo.*

Driving a big truck at night without lights *does* draw attention, though. The cops took one look at me, and hauled me off to jail in handcuffs.

In the morning, Glenn bailed me out. But instead of taking me home, he took me straight to a psychiatrist. My parents were there, and waited outside while I sat in an overstuffed chair and let this goof bombard me with questions. This was a joke. I'd go along with his stupid little test and humor everyone.

When the psychiatrist left me and went out to the waiting room, he looked my parents straight in the eye. "He's a time bomb. He's delusional, and dangerous to himself and others. I'd like you to give me permission to have him committed immediately."

The doctor was discussing shock therapy with my folks. When I overheard, Mom was resisting—and I was out of there. I made a break for it.

I was arrested in some nice neighborhood. Where was I? I didn't know.

Someone called the police on me, I suppose just because I was hanging around—not to mention the way I looked. A good call on their part, because I was there to steal.

"You need to move along, buddy," one of the officers said.

Geronimo did what he wanted *when* he wanted. "Go to hell."

That got me thrown to the ground, with my face ground into the asphalt and my arms handcuffed behind my back. No amount of questioning got them anywhere, though. Geronimo was silent as stone.

Until I was in the cruiser. As we drove down the highway, I leaned forward until my face was inches from one officer's head. Then I exploded, like a screaming war eagle.

Both guys jumped out of their skin.

I'm out of jail. I go to a friend's house. They catch me stealing. We fight.

I'm at another party. Drugs are giving me superhuman power. Staring at a fire in the fireplace, I will one black, burned-out ember to burst into flame again. My power is awesome. A guy walks by me at random and says, "That's the power of God."

Out in the cold night, I'm barefoot. Something I did got me in another fight. After I split the guy's lip, I leave. Now my feet are freezing. I think: If God has power, let Him make my feet warm.

My feet get warm. Or is it delusion?

I'm lost. I'm found. I'm everywhere. I'm nowhere.

I show up at my parents' trailer outside Boston. Mom's face changes from worried to monstrous. Dad looks grotesque to me, then just sad.

"I can spit on you," I tell them. "My spit is poison, and you'll die."

Then I find an old Grateful Dead album and turn it on at top volume, staring at my parents, daring them to try and turn it down.

The room I woke up in was institutional green. A state hospital? I didn't know, but it had that look and smell. If so, I was here to deliver all the poor inmates—the people who were *really* sane, as opposed to all these staring doctors and nurses with their stupid ideas about life and reality. *They* were the nuts here.

This was just like *One Flew Over the Cuckoo's Nest* and I was the star.

Unhappy Reality

By fragments, actual reality came back together. Unhappy reality.

When I woke up the first morning, you couldn't say I was exactly straight. But I wasn't as high. When the nurse came to give me meds, I went along with it… tucked the pill beside my cheek and swigged the water.

Later, with the pill flushed down the toilet, I sauntered over to the nurses' station. For a few minutes I chatted it up, while a nurse sat writing notes on stacks of reports. Mellow. That's how I played it. After a while I said, "Okay, so the test is pretty much over, right? I mean, I can go now—right?"

"You can talk to your doctor," she said, not even looking up.

"I don't want to talk to the doctor," I shot back, a little irritated. "Where am I, anyway?"

"Westborough State Hospital," she said, still writing.

"What am I doing here? I don't wanna be here. Was I arrested?"

"No," she said blandly, "not arrested." The *scritch-scratching* of her pencil and her "I'm busy" attitude were making me angry now. "But you're not here on your own will, either."

Rage and "Geronimo power" blew up inside me. I began shouting and roaring.

Turning, I ran down the ward. At the far end were some windows, and I barreled straight toward them at full speed. With a leap, I covered my face with my arms and I threw myself headfirst at the glass.

And just about knocked myself cold. How was I supposed to know this glass was thick and reinforced?

I'd no sooner hit the floor when two huge orderlies, like gorillas, were on me. My head roaring with pain, I began swinging. But they floored me again, with someone's huge knee crushing me to the tile.

The next thing I knew, I was in a locked room, restrained to a bed.

It was also the last thing I knew clearly for a good while.

Again there was no night or day. Only cycles. I rode up and down the onslaught of heavy sedatives. I'd start to come up to the light, and I'd go crazy, delirious. They'd come at me with a needle and I'd thrash and curse, feeling the sting in my arm. And I'd sink back into the dull darkness again.

I felt like I'd been abandoned to the pit.

Gradually, the doctors eased me off medications. I learned that at the time I'd come, I was in very bad shape. The level of drugs in my blood had been way off the scale. Between not eating or sleeping, my body was depleted. "You should have been in a body bag," one doctor said.

I'd calmed down enough that the restraints were gone. At least the ones on my physical person. Now the full reality of where I was crashed in around me. The walls. The locked doors. The truly insane, permanently delusional people I was now "free" to mingle with on the ward. And there was the "sentence"—I'd be here until a doctor decided I was okay.

To me, this might as well have been a life sentence.

If they're going to hold me here for a while, with these real nut jobs, I will *go crazy,* I thought. Even at this point, I knew only one thing to do.

I got to get some drugs. It's the only way I'll get through this.

The friend who got me liquor had no idea what alcohol would do when it mixed with the medications I was on. When it hit my blood, my mind began to spin down a black hole. That little trick got me locked up again. I'd been raving out of my mind when they found me.

Then there were episodes of violence. Once, the strong sedative they shot me up with made my muscles spasm. I contorted in pain. My jaws locked. All I could do was lay there, writhing, making strangled sounds. My temples pounded. My muscles knotted until tears ran out my eyes.

The orderlies laughed, enjoying my misery for a while. Then they gave me a second injection to relieve the spasms. Helpless, full of rage and despair, I could only lie there until the pain eased away. Sedated, I sat in a dull room, sun streaming in through dirty windows. Another day (or another week?) as a zombie.

Should I get up and go to the bathroom now, or do it when I need a drink? To *think* was overwhelming....

The day I was scheduled to leave, the doctor told me it was a no-go. He had a sense I wasn't ready.

It took another gorilla orderly to calm me down.

Back in my room, I raved and swore. Kicked chairs around. Then I opened my bag and used some of the narcotics I had hidden there.

Outside, everything had turned green after an early-June rain. I was still heavily medicated.

Now I stared out the window of my ward, letting my eyes roam the open farm fields that surrounded the hospital. Fresh air blew on my face.

Yellow sunlight was falling from a clear blue sky on new green crops that were sprouting. A guy on a tractor was cultivating.

Something in me yearned. *If only I could be free again,* I thought. *I'm dying in here.*

From somewhere inside, another voice spoke. *You haven't been free for a long, long time. And it's true—you* are *dying. Your soul is dead.*

The thing was, with all my dramatic ups and downs—right here in a state hospital—I was *still* doing drugs. It was amazing what I'd do to get my hands on the very thing that was stripping me of my sanity, my freedom, and if I kept it up, probably my life.

No Hope—No Future

The day I got out, I knew it was a joke. As I waited for my parents to pick me up, my mind reeled about the future.

I was still an addict.

Not only that, I was now a hopeless addict. I'd been stripped of my delusions. Geronimo was dead. Reality had crashed in. I was like the walking dead.

Inside, I was someplace between relieved to be out of Westborough, and scared or numb. I was no place, with nowhere to go.

Almost *literally* there was no place to go. Who would hire me? I had no money, no food, no apartment. If I had a major relapse now, because I'd been in a state psych ward, a regular drug rehab program wouldn't even take me.

When my parents picked me up, I slid in the back seat, thinking, *I'm the dregs of society. I'm the guy I've always laughed at.*

At home, my brother Glenn was visibly shaken at the sight of me. I felt every bit the burned-out mess I looked like. "I found out about this program, Rodney. It's called Teen Challenge, and they'll take you, even though…."

Which unspoken truth did he leave hanging in the air? "*…even though you've been in a nut house* ?" "*…even though you thought you were possessed by Geronimo?*"

That weekend—July Fourth weekend—I hitchhiked down to Cape Cod. With every passing mile of the highway, I thought, *I'm going no place. At eighteen, I've blown out my whole life. There's no future for guys like me. Nothing.*

At a party on a beach, I managed to get enough drugs to overdose. The group of strangers I was with left me in a cranberry bog. Probably left me for dead.

All I can remember was coming-to enough to stumble my way to Glenn's house. His wife looked horrified—or maybe disappointed—

when she saw me.

"You gotta help me, Glenn," I mumbled. "I'm done. It's over."

She let out a deep breath. "Sure, man. Whatever you say. We can get you into the program Glenn knows about."

A New Creation

July 7, 1975, I walked into the Teen Challenge Center in Brockton, Massachusetts. On the front of one building was a sign that read: "If any man be in Christ he is a new creation."

"...a new creation," I thought. *No way.* I still had voices speaking in my head. Not only that, *I've got a juvenile record, an adult record, and a record of being in a state hospital. There's no hope I'll ever be anything but a dope fiend. I probably won't even live to be twenty.*

There was a big surprise waiting for me. I'd thought I was there for an interview, to see if these people liked me and I liked them. I knew this was a religious place, and I wasn't sure I wanted to be here at all. Maybe I was just here for Glenn and my folks.

The surprise was, my family had already told the Teen Challenge people I was starting the program. There was a room ready for me and everything. I'd be one of four guys going through their program. Listless and depressed as I was, I went along with it.

Immediately, I noticed these people didn't talk or think like the people I knew. In a good kind of way.

For one thing, there was my roommate. He'd been a heroin addict for years. You couldn't miss the scarring of tracks up his arms. He'd only been in the program for two weeks, but he didn't look or sound like any heroin addict I'd ever met. That surprised me, too.

Maybe he saw the hopelessness on my face, because as I unpacked my few belongings, he kept telling me, "Rodney, God's got a plan for your life."

I wasn't ready for all this God talk, and I pulled out a little surprise of my own—the bag of dope I'd smuggled in. "Here's *my* plan," I grinned.

The guy's eyes got big. He grabbed the bag from my hands and rushed to the bathroom with me trailing after him. Before I could stop him, he dumped the contents in the bowl and sent it swirling down the drain.

"Are you crazy?" I shouted at him.

He looked at me patiently, but said firmly, "No. I *was* crazy when I was doing this stuff. But I'm not crazy anymore." And then he walked out, leaving me to stare at the toilet, thinking about what had been flushed down it:

My life, to this point.

That night, the voices in my head made a big joke out of this place. I *was* hopeless.

Over the next couple of days, watching this same guy, I knew there was something *really* different about him. All I could think was, *the sign was right—he is a new creation.*

As much as I'd craved dope, I suddenly wanted—more than anything I could think of—to be a new creation, too. But was it even possible for me? I didn't know. But I had to find out.

Alone in our room one evening, we prayed together. He helped me find the words to say:

"Jesus, let me know you're real. Amen."

When I lifted my head, I didn't know if I was a new creation or not. I didn't really *feel* much of anything. My roommate was excited, and I just smiled. Still, *something* was new. I couldn't quite put my finger on it.

Later, I was sitting in chapel, thinking about my prayer. Wondering. One of the voices in my head was mocking me. *Here's St. Rodney. Look how holy he is.*

But this time something inside me rose up and resisted. *No. I want to be changed. I want to be made new. Please, God. Please let it be true.*

And in that moment, I heard another voice. Clearer. Calmer. A voice with some awesome kind of authority somehow speaking within me. *I'm here with you now, Rodney. This is where I am. This is where you can find me.*

Then I knew, in a way I'd never known anything so certainly before. God was with me.

Something new *had* begun. A new sense of possibility.

That night, lying in bed, I realized something. The old voices were gone.

OPENING THE DOOR

Teen Challenge had let me slide by with long hair for a couple days. The rule was, short hair. Now they insisted I cut it.

"No way, man," I replied.

But they pressed me. In response, I slammed the door on the way out of the office, and went to find a pay phone.

My brother Glenn answered the call. "These people are religious idiots," I complained. "They want me to cut my hair. You gotta get me out of here. I can have my stuff packed and you can pick me up."

Glenn cut me off. "Your *hair?* You're whining about cutting your *hair?* You're crazy. You leave that program, Rodney, and you're a dead man. Do you hear what I'm telling you? You can't last an hour on the streets without going back to drugs. And this time you won't pull out of the nosedive you'll be in.

"So," Glenn went on angrily, "if you pull out of Teen Challenge, please do the family a favor. Don't come around here."

Then the line went dead.

I held the receiver in my hand and just stared. Glenn's words stung—but he was right. If I left here, where did I have to go? *The only things waiting for me outside this program are insanity and death.*

Walking back to the office, I realized just how crazy I'd really been. How stupidly stubborn I was being. Even in the face of going down the tubes, I was hanging on to this last shred of pride, independence, fighting to do it my way to the last.

I walked back into the director's office and just said, "Okay. Let's cut the hair."

That same night, I went to church again. Now something else had changed. At first I just listened as everyone sang to God. Then I saw them all differently. These were not weirdos. These people had something real on the inside. I'd been the dead, empty one. I really needed *in* on what they had.

At the end of the service, I went to the altar rail and prayed:

"Jesus, I give my whole heart to you. Please forgive me of my past and all my wrongdoing. All the people I've hurt, and lied to, and stolen from. Take my whole life, and make me a new creation. Amen."

From that moment on, real changes began to take place. Mainly, I had a new willingness to *be* changed. To admit when I was being stupid and wrong. But man, what a difference *that* made! I was no saint, that was for sure. But I'd opened a new door. And I was on a new path.

Remaking Rodney

Four months into the program, I learned that Teen Challenge ran a dairy farm in the rolling green hills of Pennsylvania, in conjunction with a school they were running.

Suddenly, I was flooded with memory—of the day back in Westborough when I looked out the ward window onto sunlight and green fields after all the darkness I'd gone through. The deep hunger for freedom and health and life I'd felt then flooded me now.

Somehow, I knew, I *had* to get to that school and work on that dairy farm.

Transferring to the farm was easy.

What I found when I got there was not.

Actually, the preaching and teaching was great. The Bible, a book I'd never read in my whole life before coming to Teen Challenge, really came to life for me. It spoke about growing in character—in things like patience, kindness, diligence, self-control. I'd never had *any* of these traits in myself before. With even this little bit of hindsight, I could see I'd been nothing but one big *impulse* all my life.

No, the farm and the teaching were not the challenge. *I* was still the challenge. If I'd thought that making a one-time decision to follow Christ was going to change everything about me instantly—well, maybe that was partly my old drug-addict's way of seeing things. As if one big "dose" of Christianity was going to ease away all other reality.

Here at the farm, it was time to make or break Rodney. *Okay, God,* I prayed. *Do whatever you've got to do. Give me the spiritual training I need.*

I guess I had no idea God would take me at my word. Or how He'd use the earthiest means to teach me the best lessons.

In the next few weeks, my "spiritual training" looked like this:

An alarm would get me up at *2:30 A.M.* Grumbling, I'd drag on my clothes and head out to the barn to milk cows. The sweet scent of hay and timothy, mixing with the sour smell of dung and urine, was sometimes overpowering.

One morning in particular, though, I decided to handle the situation by putting on my best attitude. *I'm here to learn about Christian service. So I'm going to serve Teen Challenge in the best spirit possible.*

With determination, I herded cows into stalls. In turns, I hooked them up to the milking machine. Even the stubborn ones were cooperating this morning. I was on a roll.

I was stooped beside maybe the tenth cow, sliding the milking device off her, when she began to resist. With her massive weight, she tried to knock me aside.

"Come on, you," I said patiently, pushing back. "I need this."

This time she slammed me with her whole girth into the side of the stall.

I gritted my teeth, and tried to stay calm. "You don't get it, cow. I'm going to win."

Thinking I'd outsmart her, I quickly dropped to one knee. Reaching underneath, I grabbed the milking device and started to remove it....

The next thing I knew, I was lying in fresh cow dung. Like a hockey player hip-checking an opponent, she'd banged me to the floor.

Rage blew all over me. I leaped to my feet, covered in brown stink, swearing, kicking things, shouting, *"I quit! I quit! They can milk their own cows!"*

Two hours later, still seething, I heard the chapel speaker begin by saying, "This morning, I believe the Lord has told me to talk about *self control.*" I heaved a sigh, and thought, *nailed.*

The decision to get my hair cut, back in New England, was little in comparison to the decisions I had to make almost every day as I faced the parts of me that had never developed any mature discipline. Truthfully, being on the farm was a good place for me, because I realized what a willful mule I really was. What a mess of anger and controlling, manipulating, little tricks I was—and always had been.

Now I realized that, with God working inside me, I could make new choices. Choices that were not self-centered and immature, choices to give and serve and grow little by little into a Christ-like person.

Fortunately, I was surrounded by guys who were good examples of steadiness and growth. When I heard their stories, where they'd come from, I began to feel inside that it *was* possible for me to change after all. I looked at their changed lives, and wanted that to be me.

With every choice I made to stick it out, I pushed myself further into a season of "firsts."

I didn't give up, but kept working on the farm, with the stubborn animals and the smell. It didn't matter that I was making five dollars a week. I was clean of drugs. I was not obsessing about money for the first time in years. That was freeing. I stuck with the schoolwork, too, now that my mind could focus. To my surprise, I was getting As. *That* was a first.

And for the first time in years, I felt *hope* again. I now knew I had something the world didn't give me. And the world couldn't take it away.

Rodney Hart, the hopeless addict, was being remade.

HOPE AND A FUTURE

For weeks—for a couple of months—I walked around with this full, full feeling inside me. Serving God, growing with other Christian guys. Waking up to fresh air and sunlight instead of a hangover or a craving. Could life get any better than this?

One morning, I found out.

During prayer, I asked God to come and live in me more fully. In part, it was a prayer of total surrender—*God, take all my life… every day, every minute of it.* In part, it was a sort of desperation to have and know more of God *Himself.* All I wanted was to be wrapped in, filled with, overflowing with God.

What happened when I prayed this prayer can hardly be described. It was like sun falling clean on open fields inside me. It was like filling up with fresh, clear water and feeling it spill out of you. *Nothing* I'd ever experienced on drugs could compare to this. *This* was good. *This* was what I'd been looking for when I did drugs—only this was different *and* a million times better. Not a "high," but a "fullness." A sense of being complete in God.

I kept thinking, *God's presence is with me.* It was full. Rich. This was "the pearl of great price" Jesus promised to give us. Now my hope felt complete. *God was with me!*

When I opened my mouth to pray again, a strange but beautiful language came from my lips. I recognized it as "tongues"—a supernatural prayer language, which the Bible speaks of in the New Testament. A gift from the Holy Spirit.

The Teen Challenge counselors were thrilled when I told them about the experience, which is known as "baptism in the Holy Spirit." They were also sensible enough to warn me not to let the emotions I felt take over. Ex-drug addicts *love* feelings.

Their wise counsel was to stay focused on growing steadily in character. The message was: When emotions fail you or threaten to bring you down again—and they will—it's *godly character* that will always carry you through. I felt fortunate to have spiritually mature people around me, guiding me while I was coming through this rapid-growth time of my life.

What a difference. I hardly knew myself. The peace I felt was incredible. There was just one big question that kept troubling me now. *What am I going to do with my life?*

After work every day, I'd take my Bible and go up in the hayloft of the barn to read, pray, and rest. The question about my future was always in the back of my mind. I wanted to serve God with my whole life, but what was His plan for me beyond working with stubborn cows for Teen Challenge?

As I sought God for the answer, new guys kept coming to the farm. In their eyes I could see a look I recognized. *Hopelessness.*

And at the same time, I saw in these guys a whole bunch of attitudes that were also familiar. Independence. Stubbornness. Dislike for authority. Willingness to give up and take the easy route, or even to despair, rather than tough it out and achieve. Self-destructiveness.

I thought, *man, they don't get it yet. People are here to help them and show them the right way. And they just buck authority over and over. If they'd learn how to open themselves up to God, they'd recognize that these counselors are God's servants sent to help them.*

Somewhere in there, another voice took over in my head. *Who understands all this better than a guy like you, Rodney? If anyone knows what stubborn and willful and self-destructive is, it's you. And if anyone knows how to show people the way out of that mindset, it's also you.*

Then came the big question: *Will you let me reach and help guys like this through you?*

Me, help other drug addicts? This was not exactly what I'd had in mind. But as soon as the question came, I was filled with a sense that I was on top of the world. It was right. It was God. *He has a divine plan for me!*

But how would it unfold?

After graduation from Teen Challenge, there was nothing to do but go back home. No sooner was I out in the neighborhood than old friends offered me drugs. It was like these people hadn't changed a bit. Still doping. Not changing.

I went to a party, and stayed up most of a night with them, just to talk about what God had done to change my life. I could tell they listened to my words. More than anything, they were astounded at the fact that I had not one bit of interest in the drugs they kept offering.

When I left the party, at four in the morning—without having touched drugs once—I knew. I'd really made my escape, not only *from* drugs but *into* a whole new world. The kingdom of God, where He rules and gives life.

At about that time, I also heard that David Wilkerson was starting a new school in Texas to train leaders. My heart leaped. Something inside me actually yearned to help other people escape from drugs and despair. The thing was, you didn't apply for this school. You were hand-picked by the national leaders for the program. When I heard that, my heart sank a lot.

I'd been hidden away on a dairy farm for months and months. While other guys were counseling and teaching, I was filling buckets with milk and mending barbed-wire fences, and showering cow stuff off myself. Who in Teen Challenge, besides my counselors and some milk cows, even knew I existed?

Did I have what it took to hold on in faith, believing God really did have a plan for my life? Were those thoughts I'd had about helping other ex-addicts just another delusion?

All I knew how to do now was to trust in God. He, alone, was all I had. Even if I spent my life flipping burgers or collecting garbage, I had Him.

I was still holding on—"to God alone"—when I received the phone call some time later. It was someone from Teen Challenge. "Rodney, you've been chosen to go to David Wilkerson's new school. Can you leave for Texas soon?"

My jaw dropped. How could anyone have known that was what I wanted with all my heart?

That part I'd learn later. How Wilkerson had heard about a messed up kid who'd given his heart to God and knew how to cling to Him with his whole, stubborn heart that was like a little miracle in itself.

The only question at the moment was, how could I say no?

For me, saying *yes* to Teen Challenge was a moment of destiny. It was saying *yes* to God.

God had made a way when I'd thought there was no way. He'd given me back hope. Now He was giving me a future. What else could I do but follow Him wherever He would lead?

INSIGHT FOR US ALL

Rodney Hart spent seven years in preparation for leadership under Teen Challenge's founder, David Wilkerson. Then, in fulfillment of a prayer, he was sent by Wilkerson back to Boston to pioneer a new center there. From there, he went to South America for several years to establish Paraguay's first-ever drug program, under the auspices of Teen Challenge.

Today, Rodney is the Executive Director of Teen Challenge New England, working out of the Regional Headquarters located in Brockton, Massachusetts.

I know Rodney personally to be a man of great vision. "God has a destiny for every single person who comes through Teen Challenge. Like me, all those years ago when I was totally messed up on drugs, they can't see it. But I can see it in them."

What can we all learn from Rodney's story? I believe there are some important lessons.

Words dramatically changed the course of Rodney's life. All it took was for one kid to tell him, "You were an accident." And Rodney's life veered in a bad direction.

What we can learn from this is that words have tremendous power to affect people. They have the power to discourage and destroy, and they have the power to encourage and give life.

What kind of words have affected you in your life? Discouraging words from a parent, or teacher, or a friend? If you've been wounded by criticism or other negative words, you can find healing from them by turning them over to God. In prayer, and by reading the Bible, let God give you a true and healthy assessment of yourself.

And—who is looking to you for affirmation and life-giving words? A child? Your spouse? A friend? Perhaps you need to surrender your mouth to God. Ask Him to fill your spirit with so much affirmation from Him that it spills out in the words you say to other people.

Imagine: If the words of one little boy had the power to redirect Rodney's life down a bad road, how much more do we need God's help so that our words are seasoned with a grace that gives hope and life?

There was another message that came to Rodney—and here we find a second lesson.

Rodney's parents were great people—salt of the earth, hard working. Unfortunately, they had a laid-back attitude about Rodney's marijuana smoking. Maybe they felt helpless to control him. Maybe they thought it was just a phase and he'd quit.

Rodney, like every other truly recovered addict, knows that the responsibility for his decisions rests squarely on his shoulders. No one, least of all his parents, are to blame for the years he wasted on drugs.

But to ignore, or minimize, drug use by someone you love—well, it makes no sense at all. Would you ignore it if they were holding a loaded pistol to their head? Too often, the people *around* drug addicts are left with nothing but guilt and remorse when their lives go down the tubes or are lost.

Number one: *Pray.* You will be amazed at the help and guidance God gives.

Number two: *Don't back away or excuse yourself.* Don't be one of the people who says, "I didn't know what to do. If only I had known, maybe I could have helped." If someone you know is using, *see a drug counselor today.* If they think there's nothing you can do to help, *see another one.*

Be determined to seek help until you get the kind of advice and guidance that tells you how to intervene for the good of the one you care about.

Number three: *Recognize that not all programs are alike.* When you're desperate to get help, you may think any drug rehab program will do. But remember: The goal is not just to get someone, or yourself, in a program—the goal is to get them off drugs for good.

Like some others in this book, Rodney saw several different psychiatrists, therapists, or drug rehab counselors. For most of them, the emphasis was on stopping drug use. Others dealt with important emotional issues. Not until Rodney got to Teen Challenge, though, were his deep spiritual issues addressed.

Teen Challenge recognizes the emotional factors that contribute to substance abuse. But Teen Challenge begins at a much deeper level—that is, the level of the human spirit. It's there that people encounter the terrible spiritual vacuum that exists in us all, apart from God.

Underneath it, the issue we all need to face—whether we're on drugs, or just dulling our senses in trivial pursuits—is the *hopelessness* of life when we don't know God.

Teen Challenge offers hope because it introduces people to God in a personal relationship with Jesus Christ. *Don't miss this:* Jesus is not offered as "an answer." He is real. He is present to anyone and everyone who will open their heart to Him.

Rodney was given the chance, like everyone else who walks in the door at Teen Challenge, to open up his heart and turn his life over to God. No doubt, that's been true of everyone whose story appears in this book. But what stands out in Rodney's story is a fourth important lesson for us all.

Rodney was introduced to new views and ideas about the Christian life. Just as important, though, he was given the chance to *work hard* and to *grow in character.*

Don't get me wrong. At Teen Challenge, we believe it's important to train people in principles and in knowledge of the Bible. But we also believe in training people how to stick it out with a tough job when they're tired, failing, irritated, and ready to quit. You see, that's when they're most likely to feel the hunger for that old escape into drugs or alcohol again. That's why daily chores and challenges are a part of the Teen Challenge program. On the spot, as old inner habits emerge out of daily challenges, they can be brought out in the open and addressed. And with God's help, old ways of dealing with frustration can be redirected.

Today, do you need God to help you grow in strength of character? Do you need to become a steadier, stronger person, to outgrow cynicism, despair, or an unwillingness to work?

Do you want to make a positive difference and find *your* destiny? God will help you. Why don't you take a moment right now, and ask Him to guide you?

I can assure you, He's waiting, just as He was waiting for Rodney Hart to surrender his life, and willing to direct your steps.

CHAPTER SEVEN

"The End of the Road"

— Janet —

Life is full of surprises, isn't it? Some of them are happy. Quite a few of them are not.

What do we do when life tosses us one of those dark surprises? Let's say someone you love dies tragically. Or what if the surprise is that you work really hard to achieve some goal you imagine will fill you with happiness and peace, only to find you still feel dead and empty?

Both of those unhappy surprises landed on the woman whose story you're about to read. Her name is Janet. At her request, in order to protect the privacy of others whose lives are linked with hers, we will not use her last name.

As with the other stories we've presented thus far, Janet's contains some common experiences—and some universal truths—that can speak to us all. It will also present you with questions. In particular, what do you do when life presents you with confusing or hurtful realities you don't know how to deal with? What happens when the nice surface of life cracks, and things are not "okay" anymore?

Where do you go then, and what do you do?

I believe that as you read Janet's story, you will come to the same conclusion she reached after spending a lot of time avoiding the truth.

◆ ◆ ◆

Meet Janet

Squeaky clean. That's what you would have seen if you'd looked at my family. We were definitely one of those middle-class families where "everything is okay."

Even when it wasn't.

Growing up in the 1950s and 1960s the way I did, Mom and Dad gave me some pretty strong Christian values. Honesty, hard work, achievement. As a teenager, I taught Sunday school because it was a good thing to do. My parents also instilled in me a drive to "better" myself.

That drive to be better was at work in my family when my parents moved us from East Rockaway, on Long Island, to Rockaway Center, because it was a better, more affluent community. Here we found excellent schools that produced students who were able to compete and get into the best colleges. Not that this was a white enclave, because the schools were racially mixed. The mix of high academic standards and cultural diversity gave it an air of sophistication.

I suppose that's the way I came to see myself, even as a teenager. A bit sophisticated. Not like the rough kids from nearby New York City, and not like the naïve kids from the more rural areas of upstate New York. By the time I entered high school in the early 1970s, my sights were definitely set on someplace Ivy League.

Beneath this veneer of upward mobility and sophistication, though, another force was at work.

Dark Thorns

Until I was eleven, I'd had an older brother. He was fifteen when an accidental overdose of a prescription drug caused his heart to stop. One day he was there—three days later, we were lowering his coffin into the ground.

The swiftness of his death, the shock of this tragedy, shattered our spirits. Not that you would have known from the outside. Sure, we wept openly at the funeral. The pain on my parents' faces was as unbearable as the feeling that someone had stuck a blade in my own chest. When it was over, we thought, there seemed nothing else to do but just "go on."

Going on, for us, meant just turning our backs and moving away from all the huge issues that my brother's tragic death thrust, like dark thorns, into the soul of our family.

There were spiritual issues: Where was God when this tragedy occurred? Why did He allow it? Why didn't He prevent it? How could we go on praying to and trusting in a so-called "loving God" when He seemed to be silent at times like this?

There were family issues, too: How were we going to deal with our agony and turmoil when nothing this overwhelming had ever happened to us before? More to the point, how were we going to deal with our individual pain when we didn't even know how to talk about it with each other?

And so we suffered in silence. We carried around mute pain and did nothing with it. Maybe in the absence of anything better, we were relying on that old adage, *time heals all wounds.*

For us—maybe especially for me—that would prove to be a big mistake.

Philosophical Answers

After high school, when I entered Bowdoin College, I was among the first women students allowed in. I was also a complex set of emotions and clashing ideas looking for a place to happen. My sophisticated air was only heightened by being on the cutting edge of the feminist movement, as I and the other incoming women strolled onto the campus that was formerly all male.

"What are you looking for in a college?" the guidance counselors had asked me. "What do you want to do in life?"

As I unpacked my things in the dorm, I knew exactly what I was here for. I was studying philosophy and government. The prevailing idea on college campuses was this: Old ideas were collapsing. Old ways of thinking didn't work in our postmodern society. If we could just create a new philosophical base for ourselves, we could forge a new society.

So I delved into Greek thinking. Judeo-Christian thinking. It was all very heady stuff for a freshman.

And speaking of heady, there was plenty of pot to help us "expand our minds." Okay, the truth was, pot was just an escape from the pressures of college. That, and drinking parties. But my focus was sports, cheerleading, writing and performing in plays, getting into the honor society. Drugs and alcohol were not the big focus of my life.

Not at first, anyway.

Even though I developed this intellectual, very-together veneer, underneath it all I didn't know *what* my focus was. In very rare, honest moments, I felt incredibly insecure, intimidated by most of the rest of my fellow students, who generally came from wealthy families.

I *hated* feeling insecure. I railed at myself, and told myself I had no need to be intimidated. But I didn't know how to get rid of that bad feeling any more than I knew what to do with other big and overwhelming feelings. Like the grief that sometimes came up when I thought about my brother and where he'd be in life now if he'd lived. Unfortunately, that grief was stirred many times as we discussed philosophical issues like God, the purpose of humankind, where meaning and values come from, and eternity and death.

Without knowing it, I was building a huge cache of undealt-with emotions and spiritual issues. Feelings and issues I didn't know how to face.

During my second year at Bowdoin, something changed inside me.

At a party one night, a friend held out some small tablets. "Wanna try LSD?"

I hesitated. I knew that the stories about people frying their brains on acid were largely exaggerated. Scare stories. We'd heard that the daughter of TV celebrity Art Linkletter had taken acid and jumped out a window to her death. But I knew dozens of people who dropped acid a lot. The image I had in my head was the picture of Timothy Leary, the so-called "father" of LSD, helping intellectuals "tune in" to ultimate reality by "turning on" to acid.

"Okay," I agreed. *Why not?*

One trip should have told me why not. It was bad.

I dropped the acid tabs Friday evening, and had a horrible weekend. My mind raced… repeating words, song fragments, images… over and over and over... The sound track in my head sped up, then slowed down. Suddenly I'd be on talking jags, rambling about every subject I was studying, sure I had rare insights that no one had ever thought of before. By late Saturday, I was getting exhausted and my brain felt numb. But the racing thoughts wouldn't stop. When my friends couldn't stand being around me, I retreated to the library. By now I was into an audio-hallucination, though, and every conversation seemed magnified. If somebody whispered, I imagined they were talking in my ear. Putting my fingers in my ears didn't help. Sunday morning, when I woke up, I *knew* something was terribly, terribly wrong. The school officials knew I was on drugs. They'd called the police. I looked out the window, watching for a black and white squad car to pull up. Maybe that didn't matter, though, because my brain was definitely totally fried. *I destroyed my brain and I'm becoming a vegetable. In that case, they'll take me to a psych ward.* The paranoia was extreme.

The acid wore off, of course. But all the next week, I felt shaky. I wasn't aware that sometimes using drugs doesn't *create* emotional upset or instability so much as it *reveals* it. Quite possibly, the acid trip had showed me something about myself. Buried inside were very troubled feelings—fear of death, a huge sense of being insecure and being exposed as the only non-intellectual among all these smart people.

I say the acid wore off. Really, I suffered flashbacks. Not so much the hallucinations as the terrible, terrible feelings that had swept over me during the trip.

One evening, I'd knocked off from trying to do homework. I'd been unable to concentrate. I was drafting a report, and just about every time I wrote a sentence, I'd think, *this is stupid.* And scrub at the paper with an eraser. Frustrated, I wandered over to a friend's place, where a low-key party, more of a get-together, was going on.

"Wow, Janet," my friend said as I walked in, "you look stressed. You need a drink."

Someone slid a bottle into my hand, and I let out a breath of frustration. "Could be right."

In a few minutes, the alcohol was working its magic. I felt the tension drain from my neck and shoulders. All the leftover paranoia and insecurity went with it. *This is cool,* I thought. *I'm no different than anyone else. I belong here, and I can handle this.*

The conscious realization of what was going on here never entered my head. But in my hand I was holding a bottle full of my new lifeline.

Running

The flashbacks kept returning. Hitting me at odd moments. Sitting in class, I'd give an answer and instantly feel paranoid, like everyone was staring at me. I felt stupid and exposed, as if, intellectually, I had no clothes on.

Anxiety would strike me out of the blue, as well—sometimes a terrible feeling like something inside me was dying. Like a pit of sadness and despair would open up and swallow me if I stopped all the running and busyness.

Each time, I knew what to do. Alcohol is like water on a college campus. I began to drink in an attempt to run from the flashbacks and the riot of feelings going on inside me. First it took only one drink, then a couple, but alcohol slowed me down. Made me calm.

Not once did it occur to me to seek a different kind of help.

Oddly enough, in one of my courses we were studying alcoholism. One of the symptoms, of course, is the use of alcohol to "medicate" inner discomfort. Amazing. Here I was, the young pseudo-intellectual, reading about myself and never seeing myself in the textbook in my lap.

And so, drinking and medicating, I slowly slumped into depression.

Depression is an easy word to use. How do you describe it?

Just as there are functional alcoholics—people who get up, go to work every day, and lead more or less normal lives—so there are functional depressed people. I was one of them.

I did not lay in bed all day, unable to shower or talk coherently. From the outside, you probably wouldn't have guessed what was going on beneath the together, Ivy-League-woman image. As usual, everything was "all right"—even when it wasn't. But gradually, trying to deal with college work became like mental "slow plowing." Every assignment became overwhelming. And it wasn't even that, so much as I just didn't care. What was the point?

I dropped out of college and went to London, telling myself I just needed to get out of the airless academic environment and get into real life. Some friends from Bowdoin were in London, and I hung out with them "studying" the theater. Night after night, we filled our time going to plays and productions. Through some contacts, I was able to direct some small productions. Still, somewhere way in the back of my mind, like something I'd hidden in a drawer, that old sense of death and panic remained. And I learned that I could run to London if I wanted to, but alcohol followed right along.

Now, *theater* was my thing. Once again, I had a guiding sense of direction.

Eventually, I went back to the States and wound up in New York. Bowdoin, and the pursuit of philosophy that explained life, had just been a sidetrack. Who needed answers? I loved the intensity of theater. I thought of theater—ironically enough—as something that dealt with the real issues of life. Never mind that it was all makeup and illusion and people playing parts.

With my experience as "a director in London," I was able to get work in New York theater. By this time, I was also drinking daily. Sometimes heavily. Because if I stopped drinking, the depression that had been chasing me caught up. And I hated the misery and deadness that weighted me down then. The way to keep that from happening was simple. I just never stopped drinking for very long.

TWELVE-STEP JUNKIE

Because of my practical work experience in theater I landed a job as the head of the drama department in a Brooklyn high school, in the fall of 1979.

If I'd been a manic-depressive, I'd say I was in manic phase most of the next five years. I never stopped. The school loved it, and the parents were impressed, because I produced five shows a year. It was a killer schedule.

And of course the drinking continued. That is, until I had two DWIs.

Suddenly, my little charade was over. I had to admit I needed help.

That was how, in 1984, I wound up in the Betty Ford Clinic in California.

The first thing the counselors did was to show you pictures of diseased livers. *This is what your liver looks like.* Then they showed you films, and read you information, about what alcohol does to your brain. *This is what your brain looks like.*

Then the counselors told you about the disease of alcoholism. *So,* I thought, *this is a disease.* That was good in a way. Because I'd been feeling guilty. After all, I'd come from a good home, with good values. And here I was—a lush. Among other lushes. Thinking of my condition as a disease relieved some of the guilt.

Along with this kind of education, we also went to groups and began to work the twelve-step program of Alcoholics Anonymous.

From the get-go, I wasn't a very good candidate. At one level, I wanted help. But something inside seemed to be fighting it.

For instance, we'd begin working on one of the steps—say, the fourth step. We were supposed to conduct a searching moral inventory, identifying and writing down all the bad things we'd ever done. I sat there, jotting down a few things… lies I'd told… maybe some friends I'd backstabbed with a little gossip. There were other things. I toyed with writing them down. Bit my pencil. *Does anyone really need to know this stuff? Are these things really so wrong? What's the big deal here?*

I was getting very uncomfortable.

Next to me, a middle-aged woman had begun to softly sob. I looked at her, and she burst into tears. "I've been such a terrible mother to my children. Drunk and full of self-pity, when they needed me." She convulsed in tears and sobbing.

I was at her side. Hugging. Comforting. The fourth step could wait.

Consoler and counselor. Now that was a role I could handle. People recognized a sympathetic, supportive heart when they saw one. I became "The Confidante." Self-examining penitent—well, I didn't like that role nearly as well.

The truth was, I wasn't ready for help. I knew I was an alcoholic. And it wasn't that I thought I was better than anyone else. But when it came to this idea of counting on help from outside yourself—I wasn't there yet. I believed that you had to help yourself. Sure, I believed in God. But I just couldn't wrap my mind around this idea of relying on a "higher power" to help you. Getting my stuff together—that was all up to me.

While I was at the Clinic, I began telling people that my love of teaching had worn off. The truth was, I didn't think I could handle the pressure of putting on all those productions again. I was nowhere near admitting all my manic work was part of the running. I decided I'd go to Chicago instead. It was good to get away from my old scene. All I was doing was walking away from old baggage I didn't want to have to unpack. Too much unhappy stuff to look at.

In Chicago, I became an "A.A. junkie." I managed to parlay my "experience" at Betty Ford into something of a resume item, and got several jobs working in alcohol treatment clinics. Evenings, I rode the circuit to A.A. meetings.

Almost 24-7, I worked the program intensely—all except for the steps I avoided. Especially number four—the inventory of all my wrongdoing. And *most* especially number one—turning my life over to God.

Imagine—driving yourself to drink in alcohol rehab. If anyone could pull that off, it turned out to be me. I pushed myself so hard, I was like someone running up a down escalator all the time. All around me were people whom A.A. was helping. Drunks who were getting sober. In my harsher moments, I'd ask myself, *what is your problem?* The thing was, I didn't take the time to listen for an answer.

A big part of my problem was Bill. All right, it wasn't Bill, it was the way I became addicted to Bill the way I was stuck on alcohol. Bill was a poet and jazz musician. He was handsome. He was exciting. He was creative, and counterculture, and crazy about me.

He was also a liar, who liked to keep me on his string, telling me he loved me more than anything, while he slept around.

Bill made me crazy. Or was I making myself crazy, believing his lies when he got caught and said he'd never cheat on me again? We'd fight, I'd cry, we'd make up and make love.

Soon I'd pick up the telltale signs one more time. He'd come home from a gig as the sun was coming up, with a story about barhopping around with friends at the after-hours clubs. (I never thought to ask myself why I, a recovering alcoholic, was hanging around bars so much myself.) Later, I'd ask about where they'd gone, and pieces of the story didn't match up.

Eventually, I'd discover Bill had met yet *another* woman.

And the tears, the shouting, the fighting began all over again. And the drinking.

I got tired of standing up and saying, "Hi, my name is Janet, and I fell off the wagon again last night." So tired of it that I was coming to the conclusion that I just wasn't ready to work the program. That was all. I told myself, *I can quit any time I want. I just don't want to quit right now.* It was amazing that, tired as I was getting of my own life, I wasn't tired enough to stop running and face the truth.

Eventually, the woman who was my sponsor asked to meet me for lunch one day. Over sandwiches and Cokes, she looked me straight in the eye.

"You need to give up Bill. I've watched you for months. Janet, you probably can't handle a relationship just yet. Especially not with Bill. It would take a very strong person—either a saint or a very good therapist—to survive with *that* guy. He lies to you. He cheats on you. And the more you try to change him, the more nuts you're becoming."

Her words were going into my ears. It's just that they were going through my own interpretation mechanism first. Bill wasn't *that* bad. He was just a creative artist. They were like that. High maintenance. And I wasn't *that* crazy. I was just in love. Apparently, Miss A.A. here didn't understand creative types.

When I launched into my long justification for staying with Bill, I watched her back stiffen. She leaned across the table and squeezed my hand. "Janet, listen to yourself and all your excuses. How can you have gone to all these meetings, how can you have confronted so many other people in their lies, and sit here now and lie to me? How can you lie to yourself? Why are you fighting so hard against sobriety?"

That question stunned me for a moment. *Why was I fighting so hard against sobriety?*

It was the cannon shell that almost got through. But not quite.

I was launching into another round of justifications for myself. But she cut me off. "I hate to do this, but—Janet, I'm going to ask you to choose." There was a sad but determined look in her eye. "It's Bill or me. If you stay with him, I can't be your sponsor. I can't pretend I think what you're doing is healthy and right for you. If I did, I'd be entering into a lie with you. I can't afford that kind of game playing, or *I'll* lose touch with reality, too. The last thing I want in my life is to start lying to myself again. That could drive me right back to drinking. No, thank you.

"So—" Here was the ultimatum. "What's your choice? Bill—or the program?"

It was Bill.

Of course.

Without a Rudder

When I quit the program, I was like a ship driven before a wind. Running rudderless. I *told* myself I wanted to be healthy. That I wanted to know the truth. But I continued making one bad choice after another.

Bill remained a fixture in my life. And the clubs.

And the drinking. Slowly, it increased again. Instead of falling off the wagon maybe every few weeks, it was every weekend. Then once during the week, too.

I had a little sense of reality—enough to make me feel funny about working in alcohol treatment centers when I couldn't stay sober myself. Soon I couldn't hide the symptoms from the program directors, though. It was time to move on.

Move on? Where exactly was I going? Was this going to be my life—

when one thing didn't work out, or when things got uncomfortable, I'd just run again? If that was so, why wasn't I strong enough to get up and move as fast as my two legs could carry me away from Bill? Our relationship was sure uncomfortable, for me at least.

I wound up waitressing. When I'd entered Bowdoin College, and when I'd done theater in London, it sure wasn't in my plans to wind up explaining blue plate specials. But I needed to try and get my head together. I found I really liked waitressing. Still, it was amazing and sad—I was so head-smart about things, including alcohol and drugs. I'd been able to counsel people in the clinics, but I couldn't help myself.

For a short time, I did leave Bill. The betrayals continued, and I needed to breathe. So I returned to New York long enough to get a master's degree in theater.

Then—it was right back to Chicago, and into Bill's lying arms again. *Why?* Why, when I couldn't forgive him or trust him? The answer I kept shoving to the back of my intelligent head was, *because you're dependent on him.*

And because I was willing to trade one dependency for another. Working on my master's, the old drives to succeed and better myself had returned. Since the atmosphere in a master's program is not like that in an undergraduate program—with all that silly, adolescent drinking—I'd managed to quit. Drinking wasn't going to get me where I needed to go in life. *Where was that, exactly?* But I *needed* Bill.

I worked the twelve steps on my own. I got into herbal medicines and bought my own juicer. Being healthy was my binge.

From my waitressing experience, it was only a half step to get into catering. Okay, it wasn't theater, but there was good money in schlepping trays of food and smiling at people for a catering service. There was just one tiny problem. I was around alcohol all the time. And late in the evening, when everyone's feet and backs were aching, it was relaxing to down one from the bar table—or two or so.

This time when I fell off the wagon, I'm not sure I even counted it as a minor slip. I was being so good most of the time, with my juices and health foods. Getting a buzz on after a long evening of catering was just… *therapy.*

Maybe it was one more betrayal by Bill. Maybe it was—I didn't know what. One day I woke up to the fact that I was disillusioned with my whole life. I was over forty now. Where was the career in government I'd planned? Or in theater? Bill had kids from his first marriage—where were my kids?

And so I did what I'd been doing for years. I ran. Not that I thought of it as running. I thought of it as a "geographical cure."

"I just need *out,*" I told Bill, as we fought for the last time. "We're not getting anywhere, and I need to find someplace new to start over."

Start over, I did.

In New York, I got a job as a party chef. I did very well, in that people liked me. Putting on a good party was, in a sense, good theater—and that I could do *very* well. It was functioning I didn't do well. Pleasing people, pulling together everything from appetizers to dessert, was a lot of pressure.

So I pulled up stakes and started over again in Maine. I even began going to church, but these people were so good… and I had a past.

When Maine didn't work out, I packed up and headed back to Long Island. At forty-two, I was right back in my parents' house.

Maybe that's when it hit me. I'd run a long way just to run in a circle. Was this it? Had I been running in circles all my life—running around and around the same issues, but never stopping to deal with them?

When I was in Maine, my mother had been sending me cassette tapes of messages she'd heard at church. At first, I listened to these taped sermons just to humor Mom. But something caught my attention. Often, the pastor founded his messages on Bible passages taken from the writings of the Apostle Paul. I was struck by Paul's supreme ability as a philosopher.

My college training had taught me to think like the early Greeks. The basis of all philosophy is humankind's search for happiness. Given that we're born to die, how can we live the best life possible? In the Greek way of thinking, you look at the world around you and try to reason your way to happiness. You ask: Given all that I see—people, possessions, occupations, pastimes—which combination will make me most happy?

So, your efforts to find ultimate, individual happiness were based on searching. Trying on one thing after another. Dropping what didn't satisfy your emptiness inside, and moving on to try something new.

It occurred to me that I'd never stopped long enough to look at the very thing that caused the search—that was my emptiness. For the first time, I saw it clearly, and I thought, *facing the big void inside scares me. It has scared me ever since my brother's death made me feel so overwhelmed and empty.*

Paul did not begin where the Greeks began, searching through the material world in hopes of picking up the thread that led him through the forest to happiness. He began with Hebrew logic—which was based on the belief that God had revealed himself as the source of humankind's ultimate happiness.

"*God is,*" Paul wrote in his letter to the Hebrews. To believe this is the beginning point for everyone who wants to know how to live the best life possible. "*...and he rewards those who earnestly seek him*" (Hebrews 11:6).

When I read those words, the New Testament I was holding just about dropped in my lap. Something of an epiphany occurred, as a light came on inside me for the first time.

I saw my whole life. It was like God had always been there, offering me an answer for the terrible fear of emptiness and pain that drove me. It was as if He'd been saying, "Come to me, and I'll give you healing and rest for your empty, aching soul." Actually, He *had* said almost exactly those words elsewhere in the New Testament.

All at once, the first step of A.A. began to make sense to me in a way it never had before. I'd insisted on trying to handle all my messes on my own, in my own strength. Then someday, I'd thought, maybe I'll turn over my nicely cleaned-up life to God.

Only now, I could see that cleaning myself up was something I was incapable of doing. I'd been trying to make sense of my own life, thank you, and make all the choices that I believed were "right" for me—like hanging on and on to Bill, even when doing so made me crazy. If I was ever going to escape this cycle I was on, I'd have to admit that I obviously *didn't* know what was best for me.

I'd have to begin with a leap of faith—and turn my life over to God's care and direction.

This step—the big surrender—was, as the Apostle Paul put it, the doorway to discovering new life in God.

This time, I got it.

The Big Trade

Just before I got it completely, I went back to Chicago to see Bill. Everything in me wanted to begin this new life of faith that seemed to call me. Why did I insist on seeing Bill, seeing if *maybe* I could make things work with him after all?

Our time together was a disaster. Later, I'd attribute that to the fact that by now my Mom and her whole church were praying—"God, do whatever it takes to get through to Janet this time."

Whatever else they prayed, it worked. Instead of telling myself I could *fix* the situation, I came totally to my senses. *I can't change Bill. I can't even change myself. And for all my years and years of trying to find happiness and contentment in my own strength, I'm forty-two and still trying.*

Back in Long Island, I agreed to meet Mom's pastor. He had been involved in a Colombian drug cartel, and had to run for his life when he found God and decided to turn himself around. Together, they told me about Teen Challenge and its program for women.

Actually, I'd heard about Teen Challenge when I was in Maine. I knew they had an excellent program, based on Christian principles. But at the time, I'd thought, *it's a year long. I can't afford to take a whole year out of my life just to get sober.*

But very quickly, I was pitched into depression. *Is this it?* I thought. *Am I going to keeping resisting and running when I need to surrender to God?*

Walking into the Teen Challenge center in Rhode Island, I did feel a little ridiculous. Anyone could see I was not a teen.

To my great relief, I saw that there were a good number of... well, middle aged people like myself. In fact, in short order, I'd meet people in Teen Challenge who were anywhere from their late teens to their fifties!

Unbelievably, I put on my best face for the Teen Challenge counselors. I even knew I was doing it but couldn't stop myself because I was so used to projecting I was okay. My M.O. was, *don't look like you feel.*

Teen Challenge was not like the Betty Ford Clinic at all. To be truthful, I'd gotten a lot from my time at that clinic—but Teen Challenge didn't use the "disease model." The counselors went straight for deep-soul issues. For me, it was better.

It was also a lot harder. But then, facing the stuff that went on inside me—the issues that drove me to crazy behavior—had never been my strong suit. I was still so blind to myself. And Teen Challenge held up a mirror in which I began to see myself for the first time.

For instance, there was the issue about the program itself. One of the basic, governing rules was that we had to ask for everything. That rule seemed to me impractical, unworkable, and unnecessary. Why ask for something when we were adults and could do and get things for ourselves?

"Does anyone have any issues they want to discuss?" our group leader asked one morning.

I'm sure she meant personal issues. I offered, "Yes, I'd like to talk about the program—and the fact that we have to ask for things. Can I make a suggestion?"

In fact, I found out I could *not* walk in and change the program.

Which led to frustration.

Which led to anger, because I felt out of control.

Which led back down to the issue of trust and surrendering my life fully and totally into God's care. The group confronted me over and over with the truth: If I was running my life, God was not. And if I was running my life, I was running again. Did I want that?

I gritted my teeth, then relaxed and admitted I did not.

The idea dawned on me that I first had to transfer my trust to something besides myself. In this case, the program. Once I saw that I didn't have to run my life based on my own wisdom—that I actually *couldn't* do that—it would be easier to trust my life to God and rely on His supreme and loving authority.

Just as I was handling that, the issue snuck up on me in another way.

Embarrassing to admit, but—well, most of my leaders were people who had dropped out of high school. I had a college education. A master's degree. Maybe these people were nice and well intentioned. A lot of them came from rough places and were incredibly street smart. But why was I turning over my care and well-being and daily direction to these people?

So, one of the leaders would send me on an errand to get something or do something. I'd think, *this is meaningless and stupid. If she doesn't think I recognize that this is just a "test" of obedience... some silly little hoop to jump through... she's got to get a lot smarter to trick me.*

Which put me at odds with the people over me. And though I didn't outwardly rebel—my agreeable *act* was great—quietly, subtly, I was trying to manipulate the situation.

As the saying goes, however, "you can't out-manipulate a manipulator."

"What are you bucking against now, Janet?" the group leader would prod me.

Eventually, I'd get down to it.

"I can't stand doing something just because I'm told to. I want to know why. I want to know there's a good reason, and not just a waste of time. What's the point of all this silly '*just do what you're asked to do and don't ask questions*' stuff anyway?" I quickly found out.

"Do you know one of the leading reasons substance abusers go back to drugs, alcohol, and nicotine?" she asked. "Because they run into something hard in life. Something they can't handle. It makes them sad and discouraged. Or frustrated and angry. Or it makes them feel inadequate and insecure. They hate those feelings and don't know how to face them. So they start to look for ways to escape what's going on inside."

That much I got, for sure. And for someone with "only a high school education," this woman sure knew her stuff about addicts.

"Then," she went on, "they start to run. But it's not just the uncomfortable feelings they're running from. They're running from God."

"You lost me," I put in. How was avoiding uncomfortable feelings some big spiritual deal? "How does God figure into this?"

"Here we are, Janet," she said. "Right at the front line of faith and reason. Reason tells us that we are our own authority. We think we can judge what's good and bad for us on our own. We think we can choose what's best for ourselves without opening up and asking God what's best for us.

"So, just because we don't like the pressure we're feeling in a situation, we decide it's just not good for us. Do you see? You live your whole life *based on your feelings*... and on what seems good to *you.* You're trapped inside your own skin and your own brain. That's the old way to do things—with feeling and reasoning power.

"What you need to do is to turn to God *first,* in every situation. Before you trust in yourself, your reasoning, or your feelings ever again—trust Him to be your authority. When stuff in your life seems painful or meaningless or frustrating, *trust Him.* Cling to Him. Believe that in time He'll show you His reasons for things. And even if He doesn't show you His reasons, relaxing and trusting Him to run the plan will keep you from losing your mind again and going back to booze."

I blinked. "So, it's not only trusting God. It's staying alert to my own tendency to rebel against some authority outside myself. Is that right?"

She smiled.

I got it. Now I saw why I needed this lesson about resting under the authority of someone besides myself. Not only did I need to learn to trust others who were in leadership over me as a step toward resting under authority to God himself, I needed to know how to *keep trusting,* when everything inside me wanted to rebel against things I didn't like.

I smiled, too. I had to admit, it was actually a great plan. Where on earth did these people come up with this stuff?

As if reading my thoughts, she said, "It's all there in the Bible."

CHANGED

After that, I was ready. Really ready. One night, lying awake in bed in the dark, I said, "All right, God. I'm ready to trade places with you. I'll stop trying to run things and let you take over.

"Just—please—help me to recognize it when I turn away from you and try to figure things out on my own apart from you. I don't want to run down my own roads anymore. All my running has only led me right to you. Keep me here, at your side, okay?"

Surrendering to God is a huge step, for sure. Fortunately, I knew it was something you didn't do just once and that was it. It's something you need to do every day—sometimes a hundred times during a given day. It takes practice, because it doesn't come naturally. Especially for strong, capable, thinking, independent people like me.

Now that I got what surrender was really about, it started to get a tiny bit easier every time I practiced it.

What made it easier, too, were the women I lived with every day at Teen Challenge.

Some had been really hardcore drug users. Some had sold their bodies on the streets to get money for heroin, cocaine, or just food. Most of them had pain and losses and wounds as great as the pain I sometimes felt as I started to deal with my brother's death and a million other losses I'd sustained in the course of trying to live my life my own way. And yet...

And yet, when I looked *into* the spirits of these women, I was amazed at the beauty. Listening to a woman who'd been a homeless street hooker, I heard a woman who now had deep reverence for her body—all because she'd been taught that her body was a gift from God, a sacred thing, to be honored and cared for, not degraded. Listening to a woman who'd lied, cheated, and manipulated money out of all her family and friends for dope, I heard clear, simple honesty. A respect for her own soul and her character—because she'd been taught that self-honesty and confession of sin makes the soul a clean "temple" in which God's Holy Spirit takes up residence.

Sometimes my philosophical mind wanted to argue about *all this God talk.* What about suffering? What about the fact that my brother had died young—wasn't it unfair of God to allow that? Where was the evidence of a loving God? But at least I knew better than to let myself race off down the philosophical bunny trail again.

Instead, I would look at the "evidence" all around me. These lives that had been dramatically, definitely changed. Something greater than any one of us, greater than this program, had entered these hearts and lives and changed them. That's when I realized the big and important difference in Teen Challenge's approach compared to the other programs I'd been in. Teen Challenge did all the group sessions and the individual counseling—but far and above that, they relied on the power of Christ.

That was what I sensed in the lives of these women. When I looked at them, I saw the work of Christ. I'd come here not believing at all in the supernatural. I was a rationalist. But the things that happened in the lives of these women *shouldn't* be happening. The transformations defied logic. As someone trained in theater, I knew what was pretense and what was real. As the layers of defense peeled away, I could see honest, solid, decent women emerging. And at the center of each soul was the light of Christ. I marveled at the transformations.

That included the quiet but sure changes going on in the woman whose reflection looked back at me from the mirror every day. As my year at Teen Challenge moved to a close, I was—frankly—a little shocked to realize many things inside me had actually *changed.*

The main thing—big to me, if to no one else—was that I was learning how to stop relying on my own mind to figure things out and supply answers. Every day, more and more, I learned to face difficulties and not run from them. But facing them now meant looking at the real issues, not avoiding them. And then saying, "Father, show me what Your will is in this situation. Help me to rest and have peace in You as I wait for You to work and show me what to do."

For someone who was used to providing her own answers, that was a *huge* difference. And the peace that it brought was very different, too. The old, uncomfortable emptiness was gone. So was the "in charge" version of Janet. Many times when I wanted to push my way through a problem, instead, I'd pause, stand back, and watch as God provided answers and solutions where I'd thought there were none.

Whereas I always thought I had to run my life all on my own, I now began to see Him at work in small and great things each day. In a way, knowing His loving presence also made it easier to face that "fourth step" I'd always hated—that is, admitting it when I did wrong.

That was the other change surrender brought. I no longer felt I had to defend myself with long rationalizations. Why had I never seen how far rationalizing your wrongdoing carries you away from reality? Now I could simply say, "I did this. And it was wrong. I blew it, and I'm sorry." With each honest admission came the solid, good sense of reality and the sense that I was "walking in the light" with God the Father.

The question was, could I stand to keep living in that kind of honesty and light?

Out, But Not On My Own

The main thing I owed to Teen Challenge was this: I would never have come to a saving faith in Jesus Christ without the year in their program. I saw too many miracles in that year to *not* believe in the reality of His Holy Spirit.

When the year was up, though, it was time to move home. Where exactly was that?

Carrying my suitcase back into the old apartment I maintained in New York, something felt very different. I'd always been thrilled to keep this little place here in the city, where all the action was. Now it felt empty. In the program there were rules, a schedule, people at your side the whole time supporting your beliefs. Here, I felt very much on my own. For a moment, I felt scared.

But as I moved about the apartment, I realized that something else was very different, too. I *didn't* feel empty.

Lord Jesus, I prayed, *I need to know that you are with me. Sure, I've got a car waiting for me here. A career in theater I could go back to. Old friends. But I* can't *go back to the way I was living. Please help me. Please let me know that you're here with me. I know I can't do this on my own.*

In the coming days, I realized that the sense of emptiness actually came from all the things I'd used to run to, seeking fulfillment, meaning, and escape. The glamour of the theater and artsy friends. All *that* seemed meaningless to me now.

I sighed, believing I was home free. That sense of inner freedom and peace lasted just about a year after leaving Teen Challenge. Then, out of the blue, I nose-dived into depression.

I'd gone back to waitressing, rather than seek a theater job. In that, there was just decent, hard work. Real people. Not high pressure, glitz, and everything an act.

But slowly, I began to wonder about this very unglamorous life I'd chosen. Was all that schooling and experience for nothing? Wouldn't I be making more money in a career? I started comparing myself to the well-dressed, young professionals I waited on. I was cleaning up dishes after guys in executive suits who'd been in kindergarten when I was in an Ivy League college? For a tip, they'd leave me their chump change. Where exactly was I going?

Before I'd realized what was going on, I'd allowed myself to make a spiritually deadly mistake. By comparing myself to the worldly success of other people, I'd begun to get down on myself. Looking at where I *could* have been, thinking about what I *could* be doing, the slow, silent poison of self-pity had dripped into my soul. Robbing me of hope, faith, and even physical energy. No wonder it was a struggle to get out of bed again.

I now know I faced a major fork in the road that many, maybe most, people face when they come through a truly wonderful program like Teen Challenge. It's the major problem of "re-entry" into a world that hasn't changed in what it offers—while you, yourself, have changed. All the old, shiny lures and temptations are waiting for you. All the old voices inside tell you how much happier you'd be, if you could just get a big enough slice of the world's pie.

The fork in the road, the choice I was faced with was this: I could look back on the year in Teen Challenge and say "thanks very much" for helping me out of a jam—and go right back to taking control of my life. I could imagine that surely I'd do great running my own life *this* time. After all, I was "all better," wasn't I?

Or, I could learn how to remain daily in that spiritual place of simple dependency upon God. I could learn how to let Him direct my thoughts, my feelings, my will, and all my steps.

That was when I realized what a challenge true freedom really is. It's also when I realized that freedom and peace inside were the things I'd been looking for all my life. From the time my brother had died, I'd tried to find freedom from the terrible feelings that had overwhelmed me. The sense of meaninglessness human tragedy brings. I'd begun a search. I'd tried to find meaning, to fill the emptiness, in intellectual pursuit and achievement, in theater and performance, in an intense relationship.

As I thought about this, I realized that—for me, at least—there was another danger. I'd found meaning for my life in Jesus Christ. I'd found Him while I was in the Teen Challenge program. It occurred to me where my present trouble was coming from. I was confusing the two things. The program was not my savior—it had *introduced* me to the Savior. Along with that, it had given me many things—affirmation, guidance, purpose. A sense of inner rest from my running.

If I was going to make it out on my own, I had to find those things now in a daily, growing relationship with God. I'd been a program junkie once, years ago. It hadn't worked then. I didn't want to retrace those failed steps now.

I'd need to build a strong relationship with God that helped me stay healthy and spiritually free. Sure, that would include relationships with other Christians. But the time when I was with people wasn't usually the time I needed the most help. So staying healthy in spirit had to be something I practiced during all those minutes of my life when I was by myself alone.

How did I do that?

The first step was simple. So simple a child could do it. I learned how to pray. I don't mean great, lofty prayers. I prayed like a little child.

When I started feeling alone, desperate, sad, frustrated, angry, self-pitying, jaded, bored or restless, I just prayed: *Father, help.* I cast myself on Him, just like a little kid throwing herself into the arms of her dad.

And I'd say, *please carry this load of cares for me. They're too much for me. If I carry them myself, I'll get crazy again. And we both know what that means.*

Just that, alone, began the miracle inside me all over again. Carrying stress and pain alone was the way *I'd* done my life. And maybe in the end when I'd screwed things up royal, I'd go, *okay, God, just where are you anyway?* Now I'd *start* with prayer, and let God help me do my life.

There were other spiritual disciplines I began to work into my life along with prayer. Scripture reading, and also times of quiet listening, by which I learned to stay in touch with God's guiding voice throughout my days. Listening—really listening—I learned, was every bit as important as talking to God. It's the other half of the conversation.

And so I developed the habit of tuning in to God, not just during a few moments of devotional time in the morning, but at many points throughout the day. During those stray moments when I was driving, or between things, I'd take a deep breath, relax, clear my thoughts, and "check in" with God. *How am I doing? What do I need to know about this day to get me through on an even keel?*

By learning how to build a healthy relationship with God first, I was also learning how to build healthier relationships with people. Mainly because I wasn't looking to people to be my emptiness fix anymore. By doing that in the past—*man,* had I put my life out of whack! Relationships now began to mean honesty, mutual support, and encouragement *versus* need, dependency, and stress and strain when they failed to deliver. These things I'm finding among Christians I have grown to love and trust.

As I have continued to keep those inner disciplines intact—yes, I'm still learning how—my life has steadied out. God's presence with me, inside me and in my relationships, continues to be a growing reality. When I lose my focus on Him, my life begins to lose focus, too.

But learning how to live in focus with God is no price to pay at all for balance, peace, true inner growth, and life!

How grateful I am today for Teen Challenge. It introduced me to the God who always comes to the aid of those who need Him. Because of Teen Challenge, I am incredibly blessed. All my life, I'd run. In the end, Teen Challenge directed my running, hurting spirit to Christ. And with Him is where I want to be. With Jesus Christ, I have new life.

◆◆◆

INSIGHT FOR US ALL

Some of the lessons we could take from Janet's story fit a pattern we've already seen in the stories of others. Lessons about hiding from anguish instead of facing it. Lessons about rebelling against authority and ultimately, against God.

Janet's story in particular illustrates an all too human fact. Most of us find some way to run from things that are uncomfortable to us. Drug addicts choose drugs to medicate pain. Others choose alcohol. But our escape doesn't have to be into substance abuse. Some of the rest of us choose things like success, sports, romantic relationships, hobbies, television.

Personally, I know businessmen who can boast of great success and great wealth—and yet they're no more successful at dealing honestly with the spiritual issues that drive them to certain excesses than the guy in the gutter. I also know people from all walks of life whose drug, like Janet's, is "intellectualism." They *use* their intellect to run from God, the ultimate reality, the way a heroin addict uses heroin to run from the reality of life's daily grind.

What about you? Are you missing out on real life? Living, but not *really* fully alive? What are you "using" to run from the ultimate reality of God himself?

Maybe you're not addicted to drugs or alcohol, and yet *life* is missing from your life. You don't need to keep running from one thing to another to find it any longer. As Janet and the others whose stories appear here discovered, God is waiting for you to come to Him right now, right where you are. If you need to find new life in God, take a moment to pray this prayer of invitation:

Lord Jesus Christ, I am in the snare of the devil and in bondage to drugs. I cannot help myself. The end of the road is a terrible and early death. I know that You are there and that Your heart grieves over my sin and bondage. I just can't help myself!

I want to make You Lord of my life. I renounce all sin and drugs, and want to live the rest of my life for You. Please have mercy on me and deliver me from this present evil. I do not merit Your salvation, but I accept it gratefully and unconditionally.

Thank you, Lord, for hearing my prayer. Amen.

If you prayed this prayer, we at Teen Challenge in New England want to hear from you.

There is a final important lesson for us all in Janet's story. Don't miss this.

Even when we think we've finally got our lives together, even if we're Christians, we can easily slide back into the human pattern of avoiding uncomfortable realities we don't like to deal with. In the previous chapter, Rodney Hart spoke of experiencing baptism in the Holy Spirit. Even that, important as it is, doesn't guarantee that we'll continue growing in spiritual maturity—which requires constant honesty with God and ourselves.

Teen Challenge works to prepare people for life outside of a great program that helps pattern people for spiritual health and growth. Some people find it easier to continue strong in spirit if they remain involved in a program. But for some that's not possible.

From Janet we learn that there are things we can all do to stay in the kind of close contact with God that keeps us strong and growing in spirit. These things include:

1) **Keeping an attitude of childlike trust in God**
2) **Prayer**
3) **Learning to receive guidance and direction from God—mainly through reading the Bible, and also through**

listening to Him speak to you by His Holy Spirit

4) **Good fellowship with other believers with whom you can give and receive support and encouragement**
5) **Allowing God to direct you to the kind of service that gives meaning and fulfillment to your life**

On that final point—if God has touched your heart through this book about the work of Teen Challenge in New England, ask Him in prayer if there is some way He may be calling you to serve Him by helping in our work. If so, contact us, and we'll be happy to tell you how you can be a part of what we're doing as God uses us to touch and transform lives.

Epilogue

There you have the heart of Teen Challenge: true life testimonies of miracles and changed lives. We heard from Jimmy, Lynn, Floyd, Josh, Tom, Rodney, and Janet. Each of them is a walking miracle and testament to God's grace.

Each one *overcame*—but not by their own strength, because that was long gone. Not one of them had an ounce of willpower left to quit and walk away from drugs. It was also not through a government program or a substitute addiction to another substance, like methadone, both of which have low success rates.

Rather, each one overcame by surrendering his or her life to the Lordship of Jesus Christ and to letting their lives be remade according to His new plan. They were made strong in weakness; they were delivered from the bondage of drugs by the One who has overcome both sin and death.

The Bible tells us those who come alive in Christ will be strong in spirit. It tells us,

> They overcame… by the blood of the Lamb and by the word of their testimony. (REVELATION 12:11)

It has been said, and I believe, that there are three basic plans for the life of each of us.

First: The Devil's Plan. This plan is short, ugly, and ends in an early death. This is the path that each of those who shared their stories in this book was on before their lives were completely changed by God's amazing grace.

Second: Your Own Plan. This plan amounts to wanting to do things your own way without God's help or guidance. It never leads to fulfillment. This plan includes many bumps and disappointments. Most often, choosing this plan eventually leads you into the first plan.

Third: God's Plan. Yes, God has a plan for your life. Amazing, isn't it, that out of approximately six billion people presently on earth, God knows and loves you! And He has a plan for your life. This plan is full of joy and peace in the midst of life's challenges. Following God's plan will give your life purpose, meaning, and fulfillment. This is the plan that each of the people you've read about eventually found.

Each one decided to surrender to God and to seek His will. Certainly there was overwhelming evidence that their own plans had deteriorated into a living hell, the devil's plan. That is one common thread in these stories. Here is another:

> Whoever finds his life will lose it, and whoever loses his life for my sake will find it. (MATTHEW 10:39)

Just as each one nearly lost their life to drugs and death, each one found incredible new life in spirit by turning to Christ.

We have not written this book for profit or entertainment. These true stories are recounted here for the glory of God, who reached down and mercifully saved these precious lives. Our sincere hope is that these testimonies might help others avoid or escape the misery of drugs' living hell.

In closing, we offer this book to all those smoking, snorting, or shooting death into their bodies—and to those who love them and agonize to see them free:

That all may know that God has a plan for their lives, and He loves them more than they can ever fully know.

That all may know the bondage and living death of drugs can be overcome through surrender, not to the chemicals, but to the Lord God who created each and every one.

That all may find strength to believe, or to overcome addiction through the power of the proven cure for the drug epidemic—Teen Challenge.

◆◆◆

If you have accepted Jesus as your Lord after reading this book, or would like more information about Teen Challenge, we'd like to hear from you. Please contact us at:

Teen Challenge New England Regional Headquarters
1315 Main Street
Brockton, MA 02301
(508) 586-1494
(508) 580-4186 (Fax)
Email: RBHart44@aol.com

If you're reading this book and you have an addiction to drugs or alcohol, we invite you to contact Teen Challenge. Don't put it off. Do it today.

Teen Challenge New England Centers:

CONNECTICUT
Teen Challenge Men's Center
P.O. Box 9492
New Haven, CT 06534
(203) 789-6172
Email: tcnh@comcast.net
Male Age 17 and over

Teen Challenge Women's Center
475 Howard Avenue
New Haven, CT 06519
(203) 773-1045
Email: saynoladies@tcnh.org
Female Age 17 and over

MASSACHUSETTS

Teen Challenge Men's Center
1315 Main Street
Brockton, MA 02301
(508) 586-1494
(508) 586-0667 (Fax)
Email: pastorlilley@earthlink.net
Male Age 17 and over

Teen Challenge Men's Center
9 Bloomfield Street
Dorchester, MA 02124
(617) 825-3918
Email: rjfulton@fnol.net
Male Age 17 and over

NEW HAMPSHIRE

Teen Challenge Men's Center
130 Conant Street
Manchester, NH 03102
(603) 647-7770
Email: tcmanchester@juno.com
Male Age 17 and over

RHODE ISLAND

Teen Challenge Women's Center
572 Elmwood Avenue
Providence, RI 02907
(401) 467-2970
Email: PRTCNE@aol.com
Female Age 17 and over